CAN WOMEN HAVE IT ALL?

The Story about Understanding and Achieving
Success by Turning
Crises into Opportunities

Dr CAROL S. IGHOFOSE

WOW Book Publishing™

First Edition Published by Dr Carol S. Ighofose

Copyright © 2022 Dr Carol S. Ighofose

WOW Book Publishing™

All rights reserved. Neither this book, nor any parts within it may be sold or reproduced in any form without permission.

No part of this book may be reproduced in any form or by any electronic or mechanical means including information storage and retrieval systems, without permission in writing from the author. The only exception is by a reviewer, who may quote short excerpts in a review.

The purpose of this book is to educate and entertain. The views and opinions expressed in this book are that of the author based on her personal experiences and education.

The author does not guarantee that anyone following the techniques, suggestions, ideas or strategies will become successful.

The author shall neither be liable nor responsible for any loss or damage allegedly arising from any information or suggestion in this book.

Dedication

I write this book to you, a special woman who aspires to be the best version of yourself. You strive despite obstacles and setbacks and give of yourself unselfishly in a bid to ensure that the needs of others are met. Unfortunately, you are often short-changed.

Your struggles began from the dawn of time, but your victory was also predicted at the same time. Keep striving. You are a winner!

All my love,

Carol

CAN WOMEN HAVE IT ALL?

On 13th November 2021, I lost my father suddenly. My siblings and I lost our hero! It has been truly heartrending and definitely qualifies as another crisis that I was not expecting at this time; certainly not before this book had the chance to be published.

I have not changed the text relating to Daddy to the past tense. However, it is still the case that I will never be able to sit with my Daddy and read the contents of this book to him, as I had planned to do. Nonetheless, in keeping with the ethos of the book, I will use this crisis as an opportunity.

I have committed to donating the proceeds from the direct sales of this book to support a memorial in honour of my father Hartlan Douglas and my mother Edna Douglas. This will be dedicated to assist the funding of education for young women in Jamaica.

RIP Daddy.

Love Always.

Table of Contents

About the Author VII

Acknowledgements IX

Introduction XI

   Why You Should Read this Book

Chapter 1 1

   Childhood Challenges – Laying Foundations for Success?

Chapter 2 21

   A Concept is Born… Being Respectable is a Key to Success

Chapter 3 51

   My First Major Crisis - Mummy Dies

Chapter 4 67

   Success is on the Horizon

Chapter 5 87

   Crisis Take 2 – Coping in a Blended Family

Chapter 6 100

   Success achieved - I'm outta here!

Chapter 7 115

   The Ultimate Land of Success

Chapter 8 132
   Crisis… Relationship cracks!
Chapter 9 153
   The Onset of the 'Junior Doctor' Years
Chapter 10 167
   Is this my Space?
Chapter 11 181
   Success is Reflection and Gratitude
Chapter 12 194
   Have I Got it All?
Chapter 13 209
   Myocardial Infarction (Heart Attack) Crisis
Chapter 14 223
   So, what then is success?
Chapter 15 235
   Can I really have it all?

About the Author

"Can Women have it All?"

Dr Carol has 'opened up' on this controversial subject as she wants to have a fresh dialogue and perhaps an answer! She has undoubtedly achieved a lot in her life and currently lives and works as a General Practitioner (GP) or family doctor in the UK.

She is an author, professional speaker, an ordained missionary, and mother to two adult sons. Her expertise as a health professional is garnered from a repertoire of over 30 years of experience – entering nursing school at age 19 and qualifying as a doctor 20 years later, following her decision to retrain as a medical practitioner after 13 years of practice as a nurse and a midwife.

Over the years of achieving the success she celebrates today, Dr Carol has identified and strived to overcome perceived and real barriers that remain stumbling blocks to all women achieving equitable status in our society, even today.

Some of these include, social status and resource limitations; death and bereavement; family diversification; stereotyping and ethnicity; perceptions, evaluations, and actions founded on human values encompassing equality issues; the need for understanding and accepting differences; structural and situational barriers including the glass ceiling, discrimination, insufficient funds, child-care responsibilities; and even the constraints of religion or family-held beliefs.

However, she has embraced her experiences which bring the realisation that life's events are dynamic, bringing accomplishments and tragedies alike. She has shown that one's perspective, strategy and execution alter the way an individual experiences life. She knows too well that Charles R Swindoll was correct when he famously suggested that life is 10% what happens to us but 90% how we respond. It is a game of give and take.

Learn more about Dr Carol at:

Websites—
www.carolighofose.com;
htttps://lydimedlearning.mykajabi.com
Linkedin—
https://www.linkedin.com/in/dr-carol-sighofose
Facebook—
https://www.facebook.com/carol.ighofose.5
Twitter—
@csi1111021
Instagram –
/dr.carolighofose
YouTube—
https://youtu.be/cjx-tU4Sn7A

Acknowledgements

I acknowledge my God – The Lord Jesus Christ as the centre of my life. God is great and must always be given His ascribed glory. To my beloved parents- Hartlan my father and Edna my late mother. Words are inadequate to express my sincere gratitude to you both.

I acknowledge the men who have shepherded, pastored and/or mentored me: the late Bishop Sylvanus McKenzie; Bishop Canute McKenzie; Bishop Ira D. Thompson; Bishop Dexter Edmund; Bishop Allan Simpson; Elder Delroy S. Hunter; Overseer Delton McDonald.

To Mrs. Oppenheimer, a respected senior colleague who is kind, gentle, very talented and wise: thank you for your guidance.

To my late friend Sis Jay (Dr. Jay Hamilton): I loved how you were funny, witty, and very sophisticated, yet down to earth and exuded ambition.

A huge thank you to every great Woman who has influenced me indirectly: Our Queen – HRH Queen Elizabeth II; Corrie Ten Boom; Mother Teresa; Rosa Parkes; Marie Curie; Mae C. Jemison; Mary Seacole; Maya Angelou; Michelle Obama; Oprah Winfrey.

Those who have influenced me directly:

My amazing sisters: Debbie and Andrea; Mrs. Millicent Anderson-Clarke; all my tutors at UHWI School of Nursing; my GP trainers, especially Dr Cathie Duncan; the late Evangelist D. Hunter; my treasured friends Dr Tracey Bempah, Dr. Shree, Dr Kiran, Dr. Rowena, Dr Asma, and Ms. Jan Seja whose kindness is simply admirable.

To my stepmother – Mrs. L. Douglas: we did not always see eye to eye, but you taught me many life lessons.

A special thank you to Ms. Eulanda Francis who is constantly praying for me. I truly appreciate you.

A special thanks to my adopted daughter Emily Paul for your creative and technical assistance; you are a little treasure!

To Simon Mold for your conscientious editorial assistance. Your labour of love is truly appreciated.

To all my dear friends and sisters including every sister in the Bethel Apostolic group of churches who ever prayed for and supported me in whatever way, my sincere thanks!!

Introduction

Why You Should Read this Book

Many assert that women can have it all. The reality is that we can't! In fact, we absolutely can't!!! In my opinion, it is even absurd to think that we can. A few years ago, the term may have been held as a source of empowerment, even a triumphant protestation for women. However, it appears to me that 'having it all' equates to 'doing it all' and that just does not sit right with me. How about you?

Let me hasten to say that this does not mean that women should not aim to achieve the highest possible goal or set out to maximise their potential. I have done exactly that! It just means that we may have to forgo some things deemed less important by us at particular times in our lives.

The concept of "having it all" is one that was made popular in the 1980's when Helen Gurley Brown, the then editor of *Cosmopolitan* magazine for nearly 20 years and author of the renowned book *'Having It All: Love, Success, Sex, and Money...Even If You're Starting with Nothing'*, sought to share her recipe for success with a growing population of single working women. Today, the concept is often used extensively to describe a woman's journey of finding balance in her personal and professional life.

'Having it all' refers to securing success in career, raising children, maintaining sound relationships, contributing to the larger society whilst still finding time to take care of yourself and looking and feeling at your best. 'Having it all' appears to have taken on different meanings over time and certainly holds different meanings for each woman and different groups of women at different times over the decades. Many argue that the concept has become redundant and not even worth asking. However, Dr Carol thinks differently.

In fact, she feels the time is exactly right to reopen this discussion as we live in an era when it appears women are finally on equal terms with men in society and more than ever, women appear to strive to prove that, indeed, we can have it all! But is this really the case? What is the reality?

There are millions of highly accomplished women on this planet because women have consistently survived, overcome and thrived due to our untamed ambitions and total devotion and commitment.

However, I am yet to identify or become aware of a woman who, without a shadow of doubt, concurrently has all she ever desires and all society desires (or dictates) of her. In other words, a woman

Introduction

who has struck the perfect balance in life. Perhaps she does exist, but I have just not yet encountered or learned of her. At the end of reading this book, I want you to feel liberated. I want you to return to the drawing board and consider why you hold the beliefs you did about women's empowerment.

What does it mean to be a successful woman? Are you still firmly thinking the same way, or have you changed your perspective? Either way, why? Do you think that you have failed your sisters or your daughters and/or grand-daughter/s if you are honest in saying that no woman can have it ALL?

If you do, then a simple solution is to show them a woman who has it ALL, that is, achieved the perfect life balance all at once. If you are unable to find this woman, then, perhaps you have proven your point and there is, after all, no need for guilt.

The purpose of this book is to help each of you define what success is for YOU; to present the reality of inescapable crises in life and to provide strategies and an example of an imitable mindset that may be embraced in realising such success.

The message for women remains: "Dream Big!" "The sky is the limit!" "Just go for it!" and "Yes you can!" However, you must be clear that success does not necessarily equate to society's notion of 'Having it all'.

Chapter 1

Childhood Challenges – Laying Foundations for Success?

Well, it all started out lopsided – at least, in a rather skewed way. A 'stush' (posh) young lady was being pursued by an illiterate young man from the neighbouring district. I know the term "illiterate" sounds a bit derogatory, but the truth is he was (and is still) unable to read or write fluently today. He can sign his name and that is pretty much it! He already had two children by two different mothers – arguably, nothing to do with his character.

I mean, it was down to culture and circumstances rather than a reflection of him being irresponsible. Really? That is another story, but it is fair to say he was a decent guy. He was, obviously not only 'decent' but also very ambitious. To be chasing her – that 'up-market' young lady from Reid Piece - was a rather courageous act, notwithstanding all that 'jazz' going on in his life. Nonetheless, he pursued and - as it turned out – conquered! For she did become pregnant.

For some reason, after she fell pregnant, she decided to move to Kingston to stay with relatives there and so, the baby was born in Kingston, at the renowned Kingston Victoria Jubilee hospital, to be exact. She named her beautiful baby daughter Carol Sylvia. Carol got her father's surname, but his name is not listed on her birth certificate – most likely because he was not present at the time of the registration of the baby's birth. This very decent, courageous but somewhat mysterious young man was called Hartlan Douglas.

However, if you know anything about Jamaicans and Jamaican culture, almost everyone has an alias or 'pet name'. Hartlan has several but he was mostly known as 'Pason', so that is the name we shall stick to. The posh young lady was called Edna – Edna May McKenzie.

Later, Edna decided to return to 'the country' (rural area in Jamaica) to be with Pason when Carol was around three years old. They soon got married and she became stepmother to his other children (now three) and had other children of her own.

Here is Carol, her firstborn. Even at this early age, she needed to make significant adjustments in her young life. To be born between two siblings - only they are half-sisters as she is by a different mother - is a rather precarious start. It took Carol some time to get accustomed to this man, Pason.

"The man", as she reportedly called him initially, was no-one to her but an unknown stranger. At the age of three years, it takes a bit of getting used to

Chapter 1

someone who has suddenly become an integral part of your life. Later, Edna and her sisters tell the story of how Carol feared her father initially, because she was not accustomed to him. She would scream and shout, "De man a come!" whenever Pason came home and made any attempt to get near to her. Once he had to babysit her whilst Edna was out.

Pason had to 'weed' (cut with a machete) the grass in the yard. The only way he could keep an eye on her was to get her to stand and watch him – which she was happy to do from a distance. However, she constantly kept moving a few steps backwards so he could maintain his distance as he advanced with his job of cutting the grass.

Thankfully, this was short-lived, and Carol soon became close to her father and has since maintained an extremely loving and treasured relationship with her beloved daddy. As I began telling my story above, writing about myself, the child Carol and my wonderful parents, Pason and Edna, the narrative began to lay out, in black and white, issues that may not have previously been scrutinised, even by me. It suddenly hit me that even in those three paragraphs may be lurking unacknowledged, hidden or even glaring factors that would promote or hinder my chances at success.

On closer examination, I realise that there were, in fact, quite a few factors in that excerpt that could be obstacles for my ability to obtain success later in life. Being born out of wedlock is still a discussion topic, even if such a deliberation is considered outdated and antiquated today. Throughout the world, this is something that is frowned upon to varying degrees in different societies. Nowadays, it is much more acceptable but still seen as something to be shunned, even on a micro level. It is certainly the case for those of us who subscribe to Christian principles, given that the Bible clearly teaches that sex outside of the marriage union, i.e., fornication and adultery, are wrong.

Hence, it is not the ideal situation for a child to be born outside of wedlock, according to Biblical teachings. Although this is the prevailing teaching in Christendom, for those who understand Kingdom principles such a child is no less valuable than another who is born in wedlock, because these children would have been chosen by God, even before they were merely conceptualised in their parents' minds, never mind before they were even conceived.

King David said in Psalm 139, "You knew me even before I was knitted in my mother's womb…" It has been asked in my hearing whether a child who is born out of wedlock is viewed in the same way by God - as if to say that certainly such a child is considered inferior.

Chapter 1

Even more heart-breaking, I have heard a Christian refer to a child born out of wedlock as a 'bastard'. I do not know whether this was done out of ignorance or out of sheer maliciousness.

Nonetheless, this is sad, even despicable and leaves much to be desired, especially when it is uttered by so-called Christians and educated individuals. The truth is that even Jesus Christ himself came from a lineage involving children born outside of the marriage union, if one is reasonably to infer that the child of a 'harlot' would not necessarily have been born to married parents.

I refer to Rahab in Jesus' genealogy. The reality is that this is how a certain faction of society thinks. So herein lies a factor that, even before I made my debut on this earth, could have been and perhaps was used to judge me. Let me be clear that I am in no way extolling the virtues of children being born outside of a stable family environment, and in particular, for me as a Christian, ideally in a loving Christian home with a mother and a father who are married to each other.

There is enough evidence to show that children born in such stable environments fare better generally. However, in the same breath, it is equally true that similar home environments can be toxic for children who have overzealous, fanatic Christian or other religious parents. In the Christian circles that I grew up in there was always the insinuation about "pastor's children". This innuendo could trigger a whole discourse – perhaps capable of generating content to fill an entire book! but I think I have made the point.

Then there was the issue of my estrangement, as it were, from my father. My mother, having decided to relocate to Kingston meant that my father was not a part of her pregnancy and certainly was not present at my birth - so much so that his name is not on my birth certificate. His not being around for the initial phase of development means that as a child I needed to grow to know, trust and love this strange man whom I was later taken to live with.

The issue of parental educational influence is also a factor. I mentioned earlier on that my father did not have the ability to read or write well. It does not mean that he did not have the potential, but this was never developed. I think, without a shadow of a doubt, that it was not due to Pason possessing a lower IQ but simply because he did not have the opportunity, or perhaps was not motivated enough as learning to read was never deemed a priority over surviving and providing for his family.

However, there are unanswered questions about his true intellectual abilities. Moreover, surely a child growing up with a father who is unable to read or write is affected adversely in some ways?

Chapter 1

Something worth discussing, I think. My mother, on the other hand, was quite academically inclined and would have done her best to fill this gap. Did these set of circumstances, lower my chances of achieving success later in life? Should an ambitious woman always ensure that her partner is equally educated? Arguably, for their children's sake if nothing else?

The socio-economic status of my parents was also a potential barrier to my success, even though they may have enjoyed a reasonable economic status in the community at the time. My father secured the opportunity to travel to America yearly to earn via the National Farm Work Program. However, in the grand scheme of things, they would have been considered disadvantaged.

It is well documented that children from a lower socio-economic background do less well. Children from the higher echelons of society are given more privileges simply because their parents have access to more wealth to provide them with more opportunities and expose them to circumstances, environments and individuals who are more likely to influence them to become successful.

Being born in a geographical space such as Kingston in Jamaica cannot be overlooked. Children born in so- called third world countries, are generally deemed to be at a disadvantage in terms of their opportunities for becoming successful on the world stage. The reasons are similar and or overlap with those discussed earlier in relation to socio-economic factors. Indigenous Jamaican parents, however, are known to 'push' their children towards achieving academically. In Jamaica, there are also national programmes to encourage the development of technical and practical skills, such as the Human Employment and Resource Training Trust (HEART) programme. Many individuals, who were less academically inclined or perhaps were not exposed to or given the opportunities to excel academically, do so under the auspices of these programmes and go on to become successful individuals.

I have, however, observed when I moved to the United Kingdom that for some reason many children who were born in the UK, even though they may be of Jamaican parentage, do not appear to place the same value on formal education as much as those born in Jamaica like myself. This is an area that has been researched and there are many factors that might account for this.

However, to this day I am of the firm belief that the fact that I was born and grew up in Jamaica and the way I was cultured and instructed have significantly bolstered my opportunity for success later in life. That, I am truly grateful for. Despite living in the rural area where my mother moved us to, which lacked basic modern amenities (more on this later), I was nevertheless amply provided for to

Chapter 1

foster and nurture my growth and development. Physical characteristics might have also played a part even at this early stage in my life when I was barely aware of it. I must pause at this time to mourn the fact that I do not have a childhood photograph! If one exists of me, I have never seen it. This sounds absolutely absurd in this day and age, but I have never seen a baby or childhood photograph of Carol Sylvia Douglas. Oh, how sad! I'm sure I've missed out on seeing a gorgeous baby girl but nevertheless, there we go. Suffice it to say that my dark skin complexion, even then, on a low level would be a potential barrier.

Growing up in Jamaica, skin colour was not an issue in the sense that most of us looked the same, we were loved and accepted and never given opportunities to realise that that was even an issue in the big wide world. However, we could not escape it in the wider society as we got older. I recall certain jobs seeming to be available to certain individuals with a lighter skin hue. For example, it did not appear that one could become a clerk in the bank (we used to call them a bank teller) with a complexion like mine. Neither would somebody with a dark skin tone like me become an airline steward/ess (air hostess as we call them).

These people working on the aeroplanes would have the opportunities to travel abroad and enjoy various experiences that would, undoubtedly, widen their horizons and positively have a positive impact upon their opportunities and outlook on life. I remember that the first time I met a 'bank teller' who had a complexion like mine was when I was at nursing school. She was such a novelty that I still remember the circumstances and exactly what she looked like. She had managed to secure a job in the bank - this might have been National Commercial Bank (NCB) - despite her complexion and despite her not looking like Miss Jamaica World with the lighter skin colour and longer straighter hair. It is fascinating, reminiscing on this!

Undoubtedly, such things are part of the subtle heritage of Jamaica's British colonial past. For me, however, my dark skin was certainly not an issue - at least not one that I would consciously allow to restrict me. Even if society were to have made it a barrier, it was not a barrier to the value I placed on myself then and now - even though, if truth be told and some deep psychological excavation is performed, it's likely that this has influenced me in some way, for instance being reflected in my hairstyles down the years.

However, it is something I acknowledge, and I am willing to talk about and defend, if necessary. In my previous book, I talked about how in my mind I was the prettiest girl in the district! The prettiest girl in the village! God knows what made me think like that. As I explained, perhaps it was because of my

Chapter 1

other characteristics that endeared me to individuals, especially the seniors in the community, which made me think that being accepted and respected was equivalent to being beautiful. For the purpose it served then, it was an absolutely fine narrative. If it helped me to forge a winning mindset because of the confidence and the positive self-identity I developed, then that is just fine. I often have a good laugh at that concept but maybe this way of thinking protected me somewhat and has contributed to my still very strong self-esteem and strong self-concept.

This is not being arrogant or having a superiority complex but accepting that I am a beautiful black woman, not to mention one of royal stock because "I am a child of God". I say this, as a Christian, quoting from books in the Bible including 1 Peter 2 verse 9 and Psalm 139 verse 14. This brings us to the glaring issue of being female. It is known that both male and female children develop differently biologically and psychologically.

Female children are known to demonstrate more tenacity in challenging situations in comparison to boys. [A bit contentious but the science does hold up!] Perhaps it is because of the differences in cultural values that are placed on being male and female the world over. Certainly, a lot of the values little girls are taught are with the end goal of being pleasing to males - for example, that we will eventually be good 'wife material' as we say in Jamaica. Inherent, in these values are opportunities for female children and young women to become complicit in their own oppression and eventually to sabotage their success. Despite these values in my larger society, as a young woman I was oh, so determined! Perhaps this was because I was the firstborn of my four siblings by my mother of predominantly girls. Who knows what I might have become if I had been of the opposite sex?

Doctor speculation! There is no way of knowing, but boy, am I glad that I was a female child and had the tenacity and the mindset that I seemed to have had from day one. In addition to being a female child in a situation that was actually loaded with challenges of various kinds, I had very loving parents. From all accounts and evidence available to me, my father absolutely loved my mother and I strongly believe that influenced how I viewed myself. Moreover, one thing I know without a shadow of a doubt is that my father would do anything and everything (and I don't mean anything illegal); he would do whatever it took to care for his family including all his children.

I can recall that when Daddy got his dinner every evening he would always leave a portion for us. This was just simply a gesture of his love and demonstration of how much he cared for us. We looked forward to having this later in the evening or

Chapter 1

later at night before we went to bed even if we were not hungry (although we usually were at least 'peckish' because, at the time, for us food was not available in excess such as most people in the western world are accustomed to). Maybe it was just our unique family tradition. It would be what we call 'Daddy's eat an' left' and we simply relished it! Even if it was only one dumpling, he would leave it and we would share it amongst ourselves. That was our norm and one that is fondly and lovingly remembered. I now look back and I think, "Oh my word, sometimes he probably wanted to finish his dinner!" But he would always keep back something for us. What a kind and selfless act. Thanks, Daddy.

It must be said, though, that his dinner was always nicely laid out with carbohydrates separate from the vegetables and the meat (protein) also in a separate plate / container. He would automatically get the best cuts. Of course, he deserved it. He was the man in the home who worked hard to look after his family and everyone made sure that he was well taken care of.

As an adult and in my capacity as a wife, I realise how much security that act of selflessness on my dad's part imparted to us as a family. We could always rest assured that Daddy, in his quiet and unassuming way, would be there and always providing for his family. My father is my all-time hero! After my mother passed, Daddy made sure that we stayed together as siblings. As a single parent, on some occasions he had to take on jobs that were not the typical Alpha role. I recall someone commenting on him going to the market alongside the women (whom we refer to as 'higglers') just to go and sell his produce for us children to survive. In Jamaica that is traditionally a woman's role and in such a male-dominated society it was commendable of him. Even though my father was "illiterate", he was a very intelligent man.

However, whatever his IQ level was, his EQ (emotional quotient) level was even superior. He is a kind, loving, compassionate man who recognised his role as father and provider for his children, for his family, and despite not having formal education and having a 'top job', he did his very best. For me, he gave us the same that a father who is the CEO of a multimillion company might have given his children. More so, he gave us love and values.

Another thing that I consider, as it relates to my father and his intelligence level is the fact that every year, he would travel to America to work as a farmer. He would either be picking apples in New York or cutting sugar cane in Florida. Now I look back and I think, "How did he negotiate all of that?" Year upon year, not being able to read.

How did he manage at the airport? Finding his way around and negotiating the various aspects of

Chapter 1

his contract? It is fascinating! However, it brings to mind the saying that necessity is the mother of all invention. My father had limitations but that did not stop him from using his abilities. As I said, they were not all formally developed but he used them to his best advantage and to acquire the necessary knowledge and skills so that he could be the best he could be, his primary goal being to provide for his family. That, my friend, is success and therein lies an example that was set for me even without my realising it.

From the very early stages of my development, Daddy was being a role model for me that would stand me in extremely good stead for the rest of my days. He undoubtedly taught me the value of hard work. He used to say to us as girls - there were three of us girls from my mother and my brother who is the youngest - but he would say to us, "you should never ever find yourself in a situation where you're dependent on a man".

True to his word, he did whatever it took to make sure that we got the education necessary or the ability to be independent women and independent strong women we did grow up to be! All that he did has helped us in no uncertain terms - setting our foundations for success. I think it would be remiss of me not to mention at this stage that I have not always been comfortable with my father's level of apparent intelligence. Certainly not with the fact that he is unable to speak 'proper' English and on some occasions has only been able to speak in patois when I have desperately wanted him to give a proper speech in the 'Queen's English'. The occasion of my wedding was one prime example. I was so unhappy with my father's speech, which I felt was not understood by many of the guests present that I contemplated removing it from my wedding video. It is heart-rending and appalling to think that I even considered doing such a thing. I now realise how much richness that added to the occasion and serves as a testament to who I truly am.

Even before my wedding day, on many occasions as a young child growing up and particularly as a teenager, I desperately wanted some kind of fatherly opinion from my father about particular matters. Even if he had said something that I did not agree with, I just wanted his opinion.

Unfortunately, on many occasions when I sought his advice, his standard response would be, "Carol, a yuh a fi know", translating literally "You have to know", that is "It is up to you". That response would leave me extremely frustrated and desperate for a father who would give me some definitive answers and advice.

That was rarely the case. I told myself that those were some of the realities of having a father who is not formally educated. However, as I mused to a

Chapter 1

friend about this being the only regret / frustration I had with my father, growing up, she pointed out that maybe there was nothing to be said and that my father may have simply been demonstrating how much he trusted and respected me, even as his young daughter.

Nutrition is another significant factor that is known to affect children's growth and development. Growing up, we did not have three 'square' meals per day but we were never truly hungry. Our dinner (evening meal) was the most stable meal of the day. Breakfasts were 'hit and miss', depending on which day of the week it was – there would always be a good one on Sundays, but lunch was almost always a case of eating whatever one could find: an orange or a coconut, a piece of sugarcane, mangoes, you name it. I recall things like cakes were treats and not a staple in our diet.

A 'hostess' cake (light sponge cupcake) is one taste that I can still recall. Such a food item was truly a rare luxury and thank God for that! We know that these are anything but good for us, if consumed as a staple and the fresh fruits, root tubers and all the other fresh things that we consumed and had access to were far superior. We were able to, as it were, roam free in the orchard or woods behind our house or around in the district and consume a variety of fruits. This did us immense good, even if we took it for granted at the time. Recently, I came across some information from a post that someone kindly sent me, and it outlined the nutritional value of some of the common foods that we consume in Jamaica without even thinking about it.

The article compared these fruits to some of the fruits that we consume here, in the West: for example, "Guava covers our daily Vitamin C needs 249% more than Grape". Staples like yam and breadfruit are very high in fibre and much more beneficial than the processed bread and rice that tend to be the substitute here. The meat products that we ate were predominantly fresh. For example, we had to chase the fowl or the chicken, that is, run after them and catch them and slaughter them (I apologise to those who are squeamish or are animal lovers) and then cook them.

Looking back, that taste can never be compared to the taste of the chicken we get in the supermarket here. That chicken meat was so tasty! The meat had a certain consistency and was just amazing. The beef too was different, and so were the pork and the shrimps and crayfish that we (mostly daddy) used to catch in the river. I can still taste them, and they were distinctly superior to the taste that I get from the same food now. Undoubtedly, the contamination levels would have been less, hence, even more beneficial. Again, even without thinking about it, foundations were being laid for our successful life!

Chapter 1

I cannot think of nutrition being an issue in the district where I grew up. In fact, it was only when I later gained my professional qualifications and worked for a short period at the TMRU (Tropical Metabolic Research Unit) at the University Hospital of the West Indies, that I came across children who were admitted for 'textbook' malnutrition like Kwashiorkor. Obesity, as we know it today, was certainly a very rare feature in my local village population. The nature of life meant that people had to be active in their daily tasks, which was predominantly farming, a lifestyle which entailed quite a bit of walking.

My own experience was that I developed quite a lean physique with strong muscular build because of the level of activities and exercise that became a daily part of our lifestyle. We did not have to set time aside to exercise as this was naturally incorporated into our mundane lifestyle. One regret I have is that I did not utilise the river that was a feature of our district/village landscape, to learn and develop my swimming ability. Swimming was very common amongst the children growing up in my district. That would have contributed to a healthier childhood experience, lending itself to success in life later. Except for the occasional splashes in the gully (smaller tributaries), I missed out on harnessing that particular benefit of a rural childhood experience.

"Your beginnings do not determine your ultimate success. Life is often not so much about the tools we are given or the hand we are dealt but what we make of them."

Chapter 2

A Concept is Born... Being Respectable is a Key to Success

Here I am, growing up in rural Jamaica - Windsor district. I told you I am of royal stock! I soon learn that it is important to be respectable. At that point I have not learnt much about being successful - that was not a concept that was featured a lot - but it was important to be somebody who was looked up to in the district.

One sure way to be respected or to gain respect was to become a Christian – Eureka! One day, I suddenly realised that all the people that I and others looked up to in the district were Christians. So, I thought that was interesting and that realisation struck a chord with me.

I began to pay closer attention to the values of Christianity and why its acceptance appeared to change the trajectory of one's life including one's social standing in the community. A young man who was hardly noticed before would soon become respected and gain the title of 'Brother' and a young woman could become 'Sister'. In fact, it was the case for any adult or child as soon as they became a Christian and joined the church. This newfound status, having converted to Christianity, would become true, regardless of the individual's educational, occupational, or financial state. Although this was not the real stimulus for me becoming a Christian, I certainly acknowledged and deliberated such a phenomenon. There were only a few people who lived in or visited the district regularly who could be said to be respectable individuals who were not Christians.

I can name them on one hand. They would be individuals who held some public or professional offices such as a councillor who represented the people politically, or a school inspector. On the rare occasion when a police officer would visit the district, e.g., on Election Polling Day, to assist with the transporting of the ballot box, I certainly was in awe and admittedly had some degree of trepidation!

I clearly recall one such individual, who fulfilled my criteria of being 'respectable' but was not a Christian. He had a lovely big mule that he would ride when he visited or passed through the district. He looked sophisticated and he spoke very well. One day, he had a conversation with me and said something very profound which will always remain with me.

I was taken that such a respectable man saw the need to speak to me, a young teenage girl, in this fatherly way and I took careful note of what he said. I believe that heeding his advice has helped me. It was sobering but practical information. It certainly alerted me and helped me to stay on guard as it was a warning of sorts. This wise man clearly knew that not everyone wishes us well in life. Maybe he had learnt this purely because of his life experiences or simply because he was privy to censored information.

He was not a Christian, but I believe that God used him to alert me to certain possible dangers which helped me to act carefully and wisely. I kept this information to myself for many years but later told my siblings who agreed that he did a noble thing. I will always be grateful to him but also thank God for using him in that way, particularly at such a formative stage in my life.

My pastor at the time was, in my view, the ultimate respected person in the district. He was the leader of the church that was the centre of 'village life'. Along with one of his sons, who was also the junior minister in the church, they undoubtedly became my early mentors in life. I dare say, almost on equal terms with my father.

Daddy provided for me the shelter, the basic things in life according to Maslow's Hierarchy of Needs; but meeting that part of me that wanted to thrive and wanted to get to self-actualization was fulfilled in its earliest time by my church leaders, especially by Minister C.L. McKenzie.

They provided that mentorship through biblical teachings, and through tapping into and engaging the spiritual component of me that wanted to be wise and conscientious as well as having an impact upon my soul, that is my mind, my will and my emotions. We fondly referred to my junior minister as 'Minnis' (short for Minister).

He not only paid attention to our spiritual needs but was also a stickler for education and for speaking and behaving well. He always insisted that we – young Christians in the church - displayed good deportment and demeanour. Those things appealed to me and he realised my appetite for challenges and saw that I was 'the academic type'.

I was the person who wanted to be that young lady who stands out and somehow it seems I was naturally so. He encouraged me and gave me lots of tips. We received much Christian teaching about the things that a young lady needed to know and, being as curious as I was, I was always asking him questions.

He imparted untold amounts of knowledge to me on all genres of subjects. I feel as if I became his protégée and learnt a tremendous amount from him. I undoubtedly credit him for playing a huge role in formulating who I have become as an individual as those foundation years of my life were critical.

Chapter 2

Having grown up with such a strong Christian influence and with my mentors being Christian leaders had predominantly good outcomes. Arguably, however, there are some negative outcomes. For example, the church that I grew up in was a traditional Pentecostal (Apostolic) church with very strict social norms and mores.

A lot of things were tabooed, and not conforming to the Christian way of life was a stigma for you, if as a Christian, you found yourself not strictly conforming to the church's teachings. In my view, the greatest emphasis was not the message that, "Jesus loves you" or that "He is a forgiving God and if (or when) you sin after you become a Christian, you have an advocate with the Father who pleads for you, hence, restoration is available to you as long as you seek forgiveness". Rather, once you became a Christian you were expected to be PERFECT and if you fell it became a massive scandal in the community.

As ours was only a small community, with everyone knowing each other, it would be 'the talk (or the whisper) of the town'. I mentioned earlier that those who are Christians were somehow put on a pedestal. Similarly, unfortunately, one could descend with as noticeable a crash off that same pedestal. One of the influences that I was very cognizant of over the years and even now speaking to some of my contemporaries, is the fact that the message of 'hellfire and brimstone' was sermonized a lot. Perhaps, it promoted fear rather than love and reverence for God.

It is my opinion that some individuals backslid from the church needlessly because of this skewed emphasis and expectation. In addition, the long-term outcome was not a positive one for many. In fact, some people emerged with a sense of being a failure if they did not conform to the Christian norms and got publicly recognised as very good Christians.

As a result of the emphasis on certain aspects of biblical teachings, some Christians embrace a very narrow, stringent, and arguably warped view on many life issues. They do not appear to understand the concept of God not expecting us to be perfect immediately but gradually moving on to perfection whilst aiming for His standard of Holiness. Such an understanding of God's words allows individuals to be able to forgive themselves, not if but when failure inevitably occurs.

This harsh and legalistic way of thinking results in people having poor self-esteem which is demonstrated in their view of themselves and even in their general discourse. These individuals are also notably, very critical and judgmental. Other people do not stand a chance if they happen to slip!

Chapter 2

I think it is incumbent upon me at this stage, to point out that I am in no way promoting living an immoral life because of the knowledge that restoration is possible with repentance.

In fact, the opposite is true. When individuals grasp and truly understand the concepts of justification and grace and grasp the truth about our Heavenly Father's loving and forgiving nature, coupled with the fact that He states clearly in His words that He will never leave us nor forsake us (Hebrews 13:5), one has a genuine desire to please a loving and kind God and serve out of love rather than out of fear. This approach, I can testify, makes all the difference in having a meaningful and secure relationship with God which is much more likely to last and be enjoyed and maximally developed.

For me, such revelation made the difference in whether I became successful in life as it shaped my mindset from an early stage and allowed me permission to fail. It would be remiss of me to claim that we were not taught the love of God and the promises that God made for us. Knowing the promises of God was emphasised a lot. I clearly recall a series taught by Minnis, entitled, "The 'I Wills' of God". That particular series strengthened our faith and belief in God. However, I do not feel that that basic message of God's love permeated the way it could have or should have, and it is my view that a lot of people somehow did not grasp that as the primary Christian message.

This was evidenced by many people in the district offering the excuse for not converting to Christianity as simply because they felt there was no way that they could live up to the standards that were expected of them. I am not sure why or how, but thankfully, the biblical truths of God's love and His grace resonated with me equally as the command to be holy and have been developed as I mature in Christ daily. Following my decision to become a Christian, I was resolute that even if / when I had fallen flat on my face, I would remain in the church - even if the most unpleasant situations arose.

As I grew in my Christian walk, I also realised that I did not have to do everything according to what I was told. I had the option to search the scriptures and raise questions and or seek clarification when I felt this was needed. I was by no means a rebellious Christian; I am certainly not a difficult/stubborn sheep to lead but I do not subscribe to legalism and I am prepared to ask difficult or uncomfortable questions. I think parents are best positioned to make a statement as to whether their child/ren are of a rebellious nature and I am fairly confident that my father would agree with my assertion above. I was never a child that gave my father a difficult time but as I had a critical

Chapter 2

and analytical mind, I would think outside of the box and would always be one to question things. These foundations of good mental discipline are necessary ingredients for a successful life.

Whilst I was growing up in the church, I conformed to the things that I was expected to conform to, including lifestyle practices and dress codes. Other expectations and stipulations included the way we cared for our hair. It was against the church's teachings to change the texture of our hair, so we all had 'natural' afro hair, whether or not we preferred to.

Some would hail such a rule in the ethos of accepting one's identity of African descent, but I would rather that such an important decision is made from choice, rather than be dictated. We battled with it regardless of how we felt. For the most part, we fared very well, becoming Masters of Creative African hairstyles and learning how to best care for our hair.

The hair problem was solved on many occasions because we were expected to wear hats to church, or at least, have our head covered. This, I dare say, became an area where we could express our creativity and we did exactly that through our choice of hats – sometimes these were very extravagant, but my take was, at least we had the opportunity to indulge in that area! Our dresses too were expected to be of a certain length and style. Our clothes were mostly custom-made by our dressmakers and so we had opportunities here as well to demonstrate our fashion sense or stylish prowess as long as those were kept within the strict confines of the apostolic dress code.

After I left the district and later went abroad to work, I decided that I would, as we say 'process' my hair, so I got a lovely curly perm hairstyle. By this time, I was 26 years old and a fully-fledged professional. I went back to visit home and attended church.

Of course, being who I was when I left the district - Youth President, Sunday School Teacher and Church Secretary - despite my years of service in those and other capacities, I was not even allowed to give a testimony in church with my 'Gerry Curl' hairstyle because I was not conforming! Can you imagine being denied the opportunity to give your testimony of God's goodness in your life? Yep, sit down professional Lady Carol. You do not conform, you lose your privileges!

God had continued to be good to me and had opened lots of 'doors' and given me numerous opportunities. I wanted to share these, but I was not even allowed to speak because I had changed the texture of my hair and that was a backsliding act.

Chapter 2

But that did not stop me from going to church each time I visited home. I would sit at the back of the church and quietly worship the loving God that I had come to know. That later changed as it eventually became accepted that 'foreign' churches had more 'liberal' standards. Fortunately, my faith is not based solely on what I was taught but rather, on the personal relationship that I had developed with my God. Even though my leaders were not happy with me and forbade me to speak, I could still sit in church.

I did not have to speak; I just carried on being me; carried on doing the things that I would do; even carried on paying my tithes to that church because I believe in that principle and the greater work that that church has always done. I believe whatever God blessed me with that I should share it with that estimable church that nurtured and helped me to become who I am, so that somebody else can benefit. Moreover, that experience has taught me a greater life principle, namely, that one does not always have to shout to be heard.

I have adopted a framework that I heard proposed by Dr Lyndon Johnson, a natural product Scientist and Managing Director of Technosol Limited, Jamaica who is also a Minister in the Apostolic church. Dr Johnson is a very knowledgeable individual, who I have always found offers practical and sensible information and solutions. He was a leader in the University of the West Indies Student campus ministries, where I first encountered him. Though I had not seen or heard him for years, when I recently listened to one of his teachings, he remained very pragmatic in his approach to handling day-to-day issues.

He suggested a framework to use when deciding how to make decisions and manage biblical issues that are not necessarily 'black and white'. It is predicated on asking oneself the following questions:

1. **Is this right or wrong?** This deals with the LEGALITY of an issue. If the answer is no, then, as a Christian or a moral individual, one would be inclined to proceed no further. However, in the event that there is not a clear cut 'Yes' or 'No' answer, then a second question may be asked as below:
2. **Is it for me?** This question addresses the EXPEDIENCY, that is, the suitability or fitness of the circumstances / issue to the individual or intended outcome. If one is still uncertain at this point, then it is worth asking a further question which may provide further illumination:
3. **Will it defile me?** This taps into the impact on one's CONSCIENCE. Can I live with the consequence or aftermath of this decision? At this point, a decision can be made as to how

someone wishes to proceed with a grey matter that requires some analysis and or introspection.

I think that is a very good framework to apply or use as a test of appropriateness when negotiating issues of uncertainty or controversy in the church community and how it may have an impact upon individuals on a personal level. Some examples that come to mind are Christian dress code; managing and caring for hair; use of contraceptives; organ donation; and divorce and remarriage.

This framework in no way simplifies the utter dilemma that some of these issues present but is, at least a starting point for deconstructing such complexities. In addition, I believe the questions speak to all three areas of our being – body (physical/natural or temporal self), soul (mind, will, emotion) and spirit (conscience, communication with and wisdom from God). There are some things that are clearly 'black and white' in the scriptures and require no debate or extensive discussions. However, some issues are less conclusive.

Despite this, all areas that affect our lives are worth talking about. These include taboo subjects that are generally shunned and would be otherwise avoided or even forbidden by some groups. These subjects are often what many people struggle with and or suffer with silently. Discussions around these issues will help to encourage people and reduce the chances of individuals being discouraged from engaging with the church as an institution, particularly our apostolic church. The church is without doubt, a good community, if not one of the best, that anyone may be part of.

The church community is important in many ways: if nothing else, to shape us into becoming well-adjusted individuals. In the church we deal with all members of the 'church family'. Some members are not always the lovely individuals that we all love to deal with but those are the very ones that help to smooth our rough edges as we mingle, perhaps in cumbersome and uncomfortable ways sometimes – just like stones in various inclement weather conditions on the seashore that eventually become smooth pebbles. We can infer that we were also, if not equally plagued with ridges and unequal and bumpy surfaces by the fact that we too become smooth in that process. Essentially, none of us is perfect – not even me!

Nevertheless, there are the lovely members who are endearing and supportive to the end in all circumstances. In Jamaica we sing the song, "No man is an island; No man stands alone …" The Bible itself teaches us that we should not forsake the assembling of ourselves and that iron sharpens iron (Proverbs 27:17). So, in essence, my involvement, my participation, my being a part of the church

Chapter 2

community have undoubtedly prepared, impacted and influenced me in a monumental way. However, there are issues that could have and can still be better dealt with in the church.

I know that there are individuals who have been hurt by being a part of the church community and this must be addressed and corrected. There is room for improvement. My teachers also became early mentors for me and played a significant role in my development from an early age. For example, they encouraged me to speak 'proper English'.

That is one of the things that set you apart as somebody who is heading for success versus someone who is not really going 'far'. I recall a child at high school who ran up to me one day in my capacity as a school prefect. She proceeded excitedly to tell me something in patois and then suddenly paused when I didn't answer immediately (I was merely listening attentively). She stopped in her tracks and spoke in an apologetic manner stating, "I forgot you don't understand patois!"

That encounter has stayed with me over the years. Her name was Molly – a very pleasant and articulate young student who, I am sure, went on to achieve great things. She was merely expressing herself in the day-to-day language, the language of the people. Any Jamaican will tell you that there are some things Jamaican, that just cannot be expressed in English, e.g., telling certain jokes. It just does not sound right, and the impact is not the same!

Patois is the language of the masses; it is spoken by most Jamaicans as the native language. Jamaican patois is also called Jamaican Creole by linguists. We used to refer to it as "broken English", which denotes a lesser language. It is a combination of English, French and some West African influences.

When I was growing up, if you were well educated or if you were learning and aspiring to become successful that would not have been what you spoke, especially if you were communicating with your educated elders and anyone whom you respected. Certainly, in these scenarios, one would have spoken using what we called 'proper English', i.e., the 'Queen's English'. Patois, which apparently developed in the 17th century when slaves from West and Central Africa were exposed to learned and native individuals in the Jamaican colonial setting, is often stigmatised as a lesser language even though most of the local population speak it.

I was gifted a patois dictionary by the wonderful Dr Frank Knight, an eminent Trinidad-born, Jamaican Psychiatrist, as providence of my Jamaican roots – maybe, more so for my children. I find it quite fascinating. My children, certainly my older one, has used this as an excuse to utter some words (or expletives) that I would not utter in patois and

Chapter 2

certainly not in English! He contends that he is expressing himself in his mother's native tongue which he is not pleased that I have not taught him. Dr Knight is quite the intellectual but very pragmatic and, indeed, a shrewd man. He correctly thought that that was a good gift for me especially when I later had children who were born outside of Jamaica.

Insisting that serious-minded students and aspiring individuals speak 'proper English' instead of patois in Jamaica was understandable, certainly, at the time and the place I was growing up in. English is the official language and as such, is the language that is taught in schools; that exams are set in and written in, that professionals communicate in: it is seen as the language that educated people use. It could be argued that patois is more of an endearing than a formal language.

It is very effective when used in arts. For anyone familiar with Jamaica's late Miss Luo (The Rt Hon Louise Bennet-Coverley, OM, OJ, MBE), when she speaks patois nobody thinks of her as being uneducated, but rather as an articulate but endearing person who is the epitome of Jamaican culture. Somebody who will undoubtedly stir up laughter in you! Nevertheless, it is not the language that you would speak if you were to attend an interview or if you were writing a formal exam.

So, perhaps, we ought to embrace patois for its values, rather than taking the view that not being encouraged to speak Patois in certain settings is a form of discrimination. I believe it is for practical reasons that individuals are advised or expected to speak English rather than Patois in some arenas or settings. I am aware that today there are intellectual pieces written about the impact of oral language and fierce arguments presented as to why it is a form of discrimination or even spinoffs from our slavery existence as to why Patois is demoted and not recognised as a formal language.

However, that is a debate to be had in another forum which I would welcome and happily be a part of. I am always open to learning and adapting where there is enough evidence to do so. Being adaptable, to me forms an essential characteristic of a successful individual.

Speaking the 'Queen's English' whilst growing up in Jamaica was not an issue for me at all. I loved the English language and still do. It was fascinating for me. I used to love to read. My mother used to call me "bookworm" even in those very early years. Whatever books I could lay my hands on I would be devouring them voraciously and I would get my little notebook and write down words and their meanings that I found interesting. I remember travelling home from high school on the bus with one of my friends, Peaches. We would 'talk words'.

Chapter 2

One of the words that I recall us discovering together was 'debonair': I felt it was a suitable description for Peaches and would refer to her as my debonair friend.

For that reason, I always remember that word and associate it with my beautiful, lighthearted, and courteous friend. Those occasions will be indelibly etched in my mind, and they have undoubtedly helped me in my academic endeavours. In addition to providing interesting and fascinating memories, they are little markers of success, even way back in those unlikely settings. Such disciplines have stood me in good stead over the years and have been invaluable.

Being an avid reader and having a love for words and vocabulary is even to this day highlighted or identified as a factor for success. Books provide information. One can learn lots of new skills, acquire lots of knowledge, learn new languages - the possibilities are endless! Looking back at my life and examining some of these qualities or habits that I have possessed and practised over the years, it could be argued that even in those undertakings whether knowingly or unknowingly, I was in fact practising self-help to become successful.

For example, even at that stage, I was deemed to be quite successful (academically) as I had the ability to postulate arguments and articulate points that many others would not have the same ability or courage to do. It was not because I was from a wealthier family or because I was surrounded by different people - perhaps that became the case when I went off to high school - but generally speaking it was solely because of the information that I had acquired through reading books.

It was because of my ability to immerse myself in a different world to create another reality by indulging in books and the benefits gained from that single act. Today, many people, especially young people, do not seem to like reading. In fact, as I have got older and of necessity, had to focus on my studies and work, I have had less time to read. Today, I am embracing audio books because I can indulge my appetite for new knowledge whilst doing mundane chores.

As an adult, it became expedient for me to have formal psychological tests done regarding any undiagnosed disabilities. It is a blessing that there are the facilities to do these things in England that I did not have access to during my formative years in Jamaica. The ability to identify things like dyslexia, dyscalculia, dysgraphia and other common learning disabilities can make a significant difference in an individual's academic and life achievements. I was found to have a formal visual-spatial disability.

Chapter 2

It affected some areas of my life in profound ways without my being aware of this limitation. I was told that I compensated for this disability over the years because of my advanced language skills. These were certainly acquired because of my love for reading and even without my knowledge had set me up to overcome an undiagnosed problem which existed: a ghost battle that I was inadvertently fighting daily.

In another setting, or given other habits, my disability might have been a real barrier for me and prevented me from achieving as much as I have. If it had been allowed to prevail without any additional abilities to counteract it, I certainly would have had a less favourable outcome. One book that I have read and read a lot and made lots of notes from throughout my lifetime is the Bible. I always read from the King James version whilst growing up.

Though the language is quite antiquated, I actually like its poetic nature and relish the 'thees' and 'thous'. Reading the Bible has helped me to understand and express myself. This was also encouraged at school when I attended high school, for which I am eternally grateful. Wonderful Bible passages, such as Psalm 139 which is one of my staples from high school, have helped me cement the concept of my identity as a deliberate and carefully created being. I talk more about this in my previous book which is entitled: "Fearfully and

Wonderfully Made..." In addition, the wonderful narratives, poems, parables and songs contained in the Bible, greatly influenced my love for reading it.

It is reminiscent of my love for words and for English literature. As I alluded to earlier, most of my reading in the last few years has been essential academic professional development reading rather than reading for pleasure. Of late, I have had a bit more opportunity because of the COVID-19 pandemic lockdown or quarantine periods. And you guessed it – I am also using this period to write! I have taken the decision that in addition to listening to audio books, I would like to revert to reading for pleasure as a form of relaxation. I realised that that is a key lifestyle component to assisting me to achieve holistic health.

The Jamaican 'Spelling Bee' may be a similar concept to those throughout the world I suppose – a spelling competition that school children get involved in. Certainly, in Jamaica, my schools were involved at primary school and high school level. At primary school, my teachers just chose the ones who were deemed to be the brightest. So, they just picked two of us and I recall spending an evening with my teacher regarding this. She simply asked us to spell a few words out of a book and a few days or maybe weeks later - I am unable to recall - we turned up at the spelling bee competition to represent our school.

Chapter 2

To this day I remember where I fell out of the competition. As you will see, I did not get very far; the word that I could not spell was 'CAPRICE'. I still struggle to remember the meaning of that word even now! It seems I have created a mental dislike for the word and somehow, I just cannot seem to keep its meaning in my brain. On the other hand, I have never forgotten it as the hurdle at which I fell. Then in high school, I was again selected for the spelling bee competition with other children who were good English students and could spell well. We had much better training sessions to prepare us then.

I did quite well; I am unable to recall exactly where I got to that time around in the competition, but I know we did quite well comparatively, though we did not win. The point I wish to highlight here is the difference that training and preparation make, even if the resources one has access to work with are limited. The difference between the primary school preparation and that of the high school preparation was evident to me even then and was duly noted. So, I did get to high school but not through the conventional way; the way that was expected.

At the time when I was in school in Jamaica, once you come to the end of primary school, there was an exam that 'bright' children would sit. Those who made the grade, would take this exam which is called 'Common Entrance Examination'. It is an entrance test to get into high school. At the end of primary school, you would either go to high school or a secondary school.

Those who are 'bright' and passed the Common Entrance, had their names published in the National Newspaper - The Gleaner. This is a big honour and you get to go to high school! And so it was that the brightest of us sat the Common Entrance Exam as is customary at the end of primary school. But oh, my word, I did not pass the exam! I was thoroughly disappointed. I still class this as one of the biggest disappointments of my life. I think that was the first big disappointment really. In terms of my personal achievements, failing the common entrance examination was hugely significant for me.

I did not get the grade and so my name was never in that paper! Looking back, I realise it was not merely about the pride of seeing my name in print in the Gleaner or about the prestige that comes with passing the Common Entrance Examination. Such an achievement represented a vote of confidence; a lifeline; an escape route for me. I only had one chance. I'm not sure why, but I think that was how it worked, perhaps dependent on when your birthday was and what age you were when you first sat the exam. Some people got to take it quite early. For me, this represented a possible lost opportunity as I knew of one and only one route to escape my social circumstances and that was via education.

Chapter 2

Only one child in my school passed the Common Entrance Exam that year. That child was my fellow Spelling Bee competitor. He had come from another school in Kingston to join our local country primary school, only weeks before the exam. I still remember his name and, admittedly, I used to think he was cute. For one, I was impressed that he had the surname of a well-known sports broadcaster in Jamaica – who shall remain nameless, lest I give away my secret.

Even more, he told me that they were related, and I still believe that to be true. Why would he lie? By the way, I think I have suddenly realised who my very first childhood crush was; I must have suppressed that all these years - as a good Christian girl! JJ, shall we call him... had come from Kingston to live with his grandmother in Thompson Town and from my recollection, had only arrived, maybe two or three months, before the Common Entrance Examination.

I think he was prepared well at the primary school that he came from. So, without sounding bitter, I believe that, perhaps, my preparation was not adequate. This would most likely be because of a lack of resources. I do know however, that the teachers were very hard working, and one cannot even begin to imagine the challenges they faced in executing their roles. However, I did not give up. There was another exam which is called the Special

Entrance Exam. This exam was offered by individual high schools, hence, it was like internal exams, not the universal national exam. I learned about that special entrance exam for Edwin Allen Comprehensive High School. That is the high school that I eventually attended. At the time, it was not one of the most prestigious ones in my book, but it was a high school. Edwin Allen Comprehensive High School was affectionately known as 'Compreh' and so 'Compreh' became my alma mater as did JJ's but that was where my crush ended.

I was one of the first, maybe second child from my district where I grew up to go to a high school. Certainly, the first female. Two other young girls won places at Compreh during my tenure at the school, which meant that during the latter part of my travels, I had the company of these two young ladies to travel with, particularly in the early hours of the morning.

I'm uncertain how many generations of children grew up and became adults in that district, which is currently abandoned and uninhabited for day-to-day living, but I was the first in the 80s to go to a high school. That was incredible and made me a kind of a celebrity in the community. The talk was "she pass exam and going to 'Frank Field'" - the town in which Compreh is located. Of course, my dad was very proud! At the time when I passed the exam, he sat me down and gave me a little talk

Chapter 2

about looking after myself when I go to high school and making sure that I did my best. I think the main concern for him as a parent then and in that setting would have been the risk of teenage pregnancy or that I would allow myself to become distracted by boys. Those were the typical things we were warned about and that were most likely to be our downfall. Not passing the Common Entrance Exam was a form of rejection and a form of failure in my eyes. Many still argue that if you did not pass the common entrance exam, you were not of a certain standard.

That is an undertone of the way some Jamaicans think even to this day. In my 12-year-old mind, it was a rejection, indicating that perhaps I was not good enough to fit into my perceived all important 'class' of academics - automatically positioning myself in a more elite strata of society. However, it was a setback that served as an impetus for me to realise the potential that I knew I had. Once I got into high school, I worked extremely hard.

As I did not get in via the Common Entrance Exam route, I was not put in the top stream at the outset in my 7th grade. I was put in class 7A4 to start with. After the first term, by the time we had December exams my form teacher, Miss Hilton (who was also the Spelling Bee coach), came in with the exam results one day. She was reading names – I think starting from the tenth position in the class.

She called out numbers 10, 9, 8, 7, 6 and 5, 4, 3, 2 and I was thinking Oh, my goodness, does that mean that I didn't even make it in the top10 and then when number one came my name was announced! I was top of the class and as a result of that I was moved into 7A1 – the top stream in the school! I remained in the A1 stream until I graduated from high school and was always a contender for first place in my class overall.

There was a male student called Samuel Porter who beat me to the top place on a number of occasions and occasionally there was Judith Findlay as well! I wonder why I remember those names – never used to consider myself competitive – could it be that I am wrong?

From then onwards, I thoroughly enjoyed high school despite the many challenges. Who knows, perhaps I enjoyed it because of the challenges. So, ultimately, I demonstrated (even if it was only to myself), that I was of no less ability not having passed the Common Entrance Exam. So there - for all of you Jamaican Common Entrance Snobs! I did not only excel academically in high school but also socially and emotionally. In retrospect, I was excelling in those areas as well even from primary school. At primary school I was chosen as deputy head girl. The principal just casually told me one day – it was not formal.

Chapter 2

The girl that she had chosen to be the head girl was one of my best friends at the time. I recall that she was of mixed heritage – black mother and an Indian father and very beautiful. She was very quiet and hardly spoke but she wrote beautifully. I am not sure on what grounds she was chosen to be the head girl but I liked her and she was my friend. Years later, I heard an adult criticising her and making remarks about her being favoured because of who she was including the fact that her mother was also a person in authority.

I was quite upset to hear someone talking about my friend in that way and thought the lady was just mean. However, now I look back and wonder whether this lady was merely highlighting one of the subtle nuances in our Jamaican society that we sometimes ignore what is staring us in the face. Oftentimes, certainly in our Jamaican society then (and perhaps now), being physically beautiful with parents or relatives in high places often gets you places.

Therein was another factor for being successful, but a more subtly embedded one that is not necessarily earned but gifted, shall we say. Not quite keen on that one but some argue that all opportunities should be embraced. What do you say?

"It is important that each of us determine what our definition of success is. The earlier in life this is done, the greater the chance of acquiring the necessary pre-requisites to make success as we see it, a reality."

Chapter 3

My First Major Crisis - Mummy Dies

Mummy became ill and never recovered.

At some time, when I was around age eight years, my mother became sick, I cannot recall the details of what happened or what we were told but certainly one would have never imagined the eventual outcome. She became more and more unwell. Mummy began to make trips to the doctors and trips to the hospitals. Sometimes there were stories being told that you would overhear as a child that cause you to wonder what was going on. On one occasion my mother said to me, "don't you ever marry a man who already has children!"

She did not elaborate but I subsequently learnt that at the time, she was convinced that factor was all tied up in the complexity of her illness – if you are able to read between the lines. There was a time when a lady in our district went abroad for a vacation. I remember it was her first trip abroad and it caused quite a stir in the community that someone her age was travelling abroad on vacation. I think she had some children living in the country that she visited at the time; hence, she was sponsored. On her return, she chose to walk via our home on her way to see a friend that she was visiting.

It is purported by some that my mother became quite unwell after that occasion because this lady brought back something from her visit that was supposed to make my mother's illness worse, and perhaps, even to cause her death eventually. These gossips did have a significant impact on us. I can remember as a child being very confused and suddenly not liking this woman who I had previously loved and respected, because from what I've been told whatever she had done, had made my mum ill. Another sad thing with this scenario was that this lady was a relative. She was a cousin of ours and here I am as a child, almost hating this woman. Looking back, I think it was ever so sad. We were told so many things – by many different individuals.

There were so many theories concerning my mother's illness as she got worse and worse with each passing day. I cannot recall any of this being confirmed or refuted by my father. Perhaps he was as confused and uncertain as we were. Nonetheless, it is beyond belief to think that we were not sat down and told something or given some narrative but that was the reality of my childhood circumstances.

This was not done, simply because it was not the thing to do. I desperately wanted to believe the stories were confabulated, and still do, but what were we to do? We were only children; we did not

Chapter 3

know any better. Unfortunately, in those days managing chronic illnesses or terminal illnesses was nothing like it is today. In fact, I am not even sure what it is like today in Jamaica but certainly it was not anything that is remotely desirable. My mother continued to become more unwell, and I soon realised that hers was specifically a woman's illness because of some of the features that were associated with the illness. I have a good idea about the nature of my mother's illness but have no evidence, e.g., in written form.

Looking back, I wonder whether she had all the screening that she needed to have had, particularly, her 'pap smear' as it was then called in Jamaica. I know the service for screening for cervical cancer was extensively rolled out and may have been patchy in areas but from what I know, she would have been able to access that screening program if she was fully aware and had the desire to.

I remember taking her 'clothes' daily to what we then called, 'the gully' which is a tributary of a river and washing them. This means, hand washing. These items of 'clothing' were not just dresses, skirts, blouses, and underwear garments; we were unable to afford sanitary /disposable pads / pants so the home-made ones of these were also included plus anything including sheets and anything else that required washing. I washed and washed and washed day after day hoping with every cell in my little body that this would soon come to an end; that my mother would soon become well again. Looking back now I realise that this must have had an additional impact on my very courageous mother; having had to depend on us children, me, being the oldest one, to care for her and in this way. How vulnerable she must have felt.

Nowadays we hear about children in the role of carers and the impact that this is likely to have on them psychologically, physically, educationally and socially. That concept of 'child carer' was not one that we had heard of in Jamaica at the time when I was growing up.

However, looking back, I realise that I had, of necessity, had to take on a huge burden of essentially caring for my ill mother and had played that role at a point in life. My father was around, and he did his very best but there were some things that I had to do especially as the oldest female child. Moreover, daddy still had the responsibility of providing for the entire family. In Jamaica, there isn't a welfare system that could have propped up his earnings and each trip to the doctor's office would have cost him, though the hospital bills might have been free or supplemented.

Unknown to me, at the time, this was yet another way of preparing me for a life that was to come. A life filled with uncertainty; a life of giving selflessly;

Chapter 3

a life of learning to put others before myself; a life of being ingenious and creative – utilising available resources to the best of my ability but also a life of adaptability, learning to embrace the moment and even have some fun amid crises. I had to do all the chores I mentioned above but I remember that even during those times, our existence was not one of doom and gloom.

We still played as children; we still got on with things like other children did. Even when we went to the gully to wash her 'clothes', we still found time to have some type of fun. I remember those days were long and exhausting and we would spend hours and hours just trying to get all the washing done. There is a famous saying that I heard quoted by Oprah Winfrey, perhaps originally coined by Martin Luther King Jr - "not everybody can be famous, but everybody can be great because greatness is determined by service.". I think even in this tragedy I was being prepared; I was giving service and learning how to serve and that has set me up to deal with every individual that I come across in life.

To be able to ask the question, "what can I do to serve this individual, to make this person's life better? What can I teach them?". Because my desire is to touch every life that I encounter. It might have been a difficult time as a child, but it has certainly not scarred me emotionally. I think of the difficulty that my mother would have had to go through. However, I am certainly glad that I was around at that time; that God had placed me on this earth at that time to have been able to do what I did innocently as a child, for a mother that I loved and cared for. I hope she did not in any way feel that she was a burden to me (or us) at any point. I most certainly have never looked at it like that. The truth is that those actions, that situation, prepared me for success in life later and more so, in many ways that my little bare-footed, country girl self, had not envisioned.

Unfortunately, my mother's pains got worse and the situation just continued. On some days she would call me into the room where she was, and she would ask me to read from the Bible for her. Psalm 91 was one of her favourite scriptures. I would read that scripture for her almost every day so much so that I knew that Psalm 'by heart'.

I can still repeat most of it by rote. "He that dwelleth in the secret place of the Most High shall abide under the shadow of the Almighty. I will say of the Lord he is my refuge and my fortress my God, in him will I trust..." The other thing that was extremely distressing was hearing my mother crying in pain. She used to experience extreme pain! To compound it all, she was also wasting away. She rapidly became very emaciated and debilitated. Though she was always a slim woman, she became a

Chapter 3

fraction of her original self. Shortly after she became unwell, we did not have a mother who could cook for us and care for us and look after us. That was a thing of the past. I remember willing everything and hoping against hope that my mother would become well just so I could, like other children, have a mother who could just be a mother to us; just so things would be normal like everybody else's mother. But, alas, the pains got worse and my mother continued to deteriorate.

One day I heard my mother crying - it was a kind of wail that was heart breaking! I still remember when she looked at an orange tree that was in front of her doorway – the root system above the ground but directly underneath the tree itself provided a very cool and comfortable seating area for us to relax. The house we lived in was almost in an orange orchard; we had orange trees all around us with beautiful, sweet and juicy fruits that we could access by stretching out or elevating an arm.

Before the fruits emerged, the trees would be covered with beautiful orange blossoms that filled the air with their delicate and fresh scent which we, almost always took for granted, but I recall the busy bees and tiny hummingbirds making use of the pollens and nectar. In all of this the sun shone radiantly as if determined to provide rays of hope for us. That were some of the many advantages we had as children growing up in the very rural district of Windsor, Clarendon – Jamaica. We could pick an orange and eat it at any time, and we tended to have oranges almost all year round but especially in the summertime when most of the fruits were ripe and at their best.

But I will never forget when my mother looked at that orange tree and said, "if I knew that death lived underneath that tree, I would go there and give myself to death and say, "here I am, take me". Those words and that occasion have left an indelible mark on my mind. When I recall those words, my heart breaks. I can only imagine the agony that she must have been going through to prompt her to say that and to say it out loud that her child/ren could hear. Oh, how she suffered!

Palliative care and pain management as I know it in the UK now is very advanced, though still a work in progress. I sincerely hope that no woman, no one, should ever have to experience such agony in the last few months or days of their life. The suffering did not stop. The wasting away did not stop.

The pain and the crying did not stop. The many trips to the gully to do the washing did not stop. My beautiful and brave mother just continued to get worse. Her sisters visited but soon it was just as if it had become the norm. There was nothing that anyone could do and on a few occasions we even thought we had lost her when she was too weak and

Chapter 3

debilitated to breathe. But one day she actually did go; her eyes closed, and she never opened them again. She never took another breath; never said another word and she never cried another tear. That was it. I clearly recall my father saying to me in a calm manner, "Carol your mother is gone".

That night we were all anticipating it. She had got so bad; we were surrounded by relatives from our neighbouring district - Reid Piece, where my mum originally came from. When she passed, despite the hurt and the pain, there was peace. By this time, her death was anticipated and even I had relented to the fact that we were losing her. It was anticipated. I remember that we all got together with some of my cousins from Reid Piece who were renowned for their singing voices, and we sang. It was a singing that I still cannot understand. However, looking back, I know I felt some kind of relief.

Though I understood that it was one of the worst things that could have happened to a child, for some unexplained reason, there was an enduring feeling of peace. I recall that even on the day of her burial I had a calmness that was uncharacteristic. I felt like I should even force myself to cry but I could not. I knew I should be crying but I could not cry. My mother had gone but I had come to accept it and the customary hollering, weeping and wailing seemed out of place for me, though others did just that. I was upset but seemingly had resolved to move on. The burial provided closure.

I remember experiencing a weird bout of hiccupping, a kind of cry towards the end, but she had gone and that was it. Now we would have to get on with our lives and I was the 'big one', that is, the older sibling. My mother's relatives stopped visiting shortly after. My aunt who had loved and cared for me as a baby also disappeared from our lives. My father was determined that we would remain together and though I understood that several relatives offered to grow one of us as part of their own families, my father was adamant that we would not be separated; we would grow up together and he would care for us as best as he could.

That is exactly what my brave and wise father did, and we are eternally grateful to him. Today, my siblings and I are a very close and a tight unit. We enjoy an enviably close relationship and support each other in every way possible. So, what did my mother die of? I believe that my mother died from either uterine or cervical cancer, but cervical cancer is more likely to be the culprit, given the general statistics and epidemiology surrounding her circumstances.

According to the World Health Organisation (WHO) 2020, Cervical cancer develops in a woman's cervix (the entrance to the uterus from the vagina).

Chapter 3

Almost all cervical cancer cases (99%) are linked to infection with high-risk human papillomaviruses (HPV), an extremely common virus transmitted in women who are sexually active. Although most infections with HPV resolve spontaneously and cause no symptoms, persistent infection can cause cervical cancer in women.

Today, there are vaccines to prevent HPV. Cervical cancer is the fourth most common cancer in women. In 2018, an estimated 570 000 women were diagnosed with cervical cancer worldwide and about 311 000 women died from the disease that year. Effective primary (HPV vaccination) and secondary prevention approaches (screening for and treating precancerous lesions) will prevent most cervical cancer cases. When diagnosed, cervical cancer is one of the most successfully treatable forms of cancer if it is detected early and managed effectively.

Cancers diagnosed in late stages can also be controlled with appropriate treatment and palliative care. With a comprehensive approach to prevent, screen and treat, cervical cancer can be eliminated as a public health problem within a generation. I urge all women to embrace the prevention and screening program to reduce the risk of this horrible disease.

What do you do when you experience such a major crisis of losing a parent at such a young age?

How do you learn to move past that? How do you manage such a crisis? I grieved but had to move on because time was not waiting for anybody. I think the blow was somewhat more tolerable because I had resolved myself to accepting losing her even before it became a reality, when I realised it was inevitable.

So, we went back to "normal" life after a few months. But before that, one of the ladies in the district came and stayed with us at home for a few days, maybe one or two weeks. She cooked for us, she cared for us and remained with us day and night. God bless her soul. We called her Aunt Doll, most people in the district just called her 'Andal'.

I do not know her real name, but I do remember that she was the wife of my mother's uncle, Uncle Eddie, remembered for his very severe stutter, hence, her surname would have been McKenzie, but that is as far as I know. I remember a particular meal that she cooked for us. It consisted of pork. The meat was cooked so succulently and was so tasty, I still remember it to this day. Andal passed away some time after my mother. May her soul rest in peace.

My sister has requested that I also include the details regarding my bedtime story telling vigils here. As an avid reader, I had many stories to tell and would indulge them recounting the many tales

Chapter 3

that I had read from various traditional Caribbean or European books. She pointed out the semblance of normalcy that such occasions brought to our precious family at that poignant time, recalling the details of one of the favourite stories that I would tell and singing the accompany song which I composed in order to make the story more engaging and entertaining. Even today, we still remember my famous "Kiteenge" song and when my sister recently sang it again to me, I could not help allowing the tears to flow!

The late Dr Myles Munroe, renowned Bahamian Evangelist, Author, Speaker and Leadership Consultant defined crisis as an event, circumstance or situation affecting you or your environment over which you have no direct cause, control or responsibility. Crisis is unplanned and uncontrolled change. Despite this negative connotation of crisis, crises are deemed to provide some benefits. Shakespeare said of crisis, "sweet are the uses of adversity". Jon Huntsman said, "If there is a silver lining to bad times, it is this: when facing severe challenges, your mind is normally at its sharpest".

Dr Munroe, further purported the following points about crisis, which I find beneficial to consider:

1. acknowledge that crisis is ubiquitous; they are a part of life and serve a purpose

2. crisis is the incubator of creativity – a crisis demands a new way of thinking about old problem/s
3. crisis creates opportunity
4. crisis is an opportunity to improve and advance over old ideas
5. crisis produces growth and development
6. crisis may produce and manifest good leadership ability
7. crisis ignites the passion of vision

It is said that crises guarantee our place in history. The history lesson may demonstrate a crisis managed well or inappropriately. The points below are worth considering if we are desirous of avoiding mismanaging our crises.

1. Operate from the premise that everything is working for our good – believe that someone greater than ourselves is in control. (As a Christian, I believe that to be the Lord Jesus Christ).
2. Do not lose heart because you do not understand the why.
3. Treat each crisis as an opportunity to present and defend your beliefs and convictions.
4. Avoid making quick judgements or decisions in a crisis, if possible – we have revolving emotions and may need additional details. Learn to Forgive.

Chapter 3

5. Focus on the solution rather than the crisis or the pain – use guidelines, including scriptures, songs, inspirational messages to refocus. Also, recall past crises and the opportunities and lessons that followed.
6. Take advantage of every crisis by learning all you can about it or learn in the situation e.g., learn about the object or cause of the crisis - people / culture / leadership.
7. Demonstrate a sense of gratitude - find something to be grateful for in the situation. Gratitude always works!
8. Refuse unscriptural / unwise advice. (No one else is you but you; despite what others say, they do not know how they will respond in any given situation or crisis!
9. Embrace each crisis as an opportunity to learn about yourself – your strengths and weaknesses, morality, allegiance / loyalty.
10. Learn how to treat people right - rejection has a depth of pain that is equal to nothing else. Be compassionate – passion should never become more important than compassion.

I recently heard Bishop C.A. Holdsworth (Jamaica), in one of his teachings commented that we will either emerge BITTER or BETTER from a crisis. I do believe that I have emerged better from this particular crisis and hope that will be the case for you as you inevitably encounter crisis/es in life.

"Dealing with a major crisis in life will either make or break you. The lessons learnt and the mindset that you emerge with will, undoubtedly greatly impact your attitude to future life events and by extension, whether you ultimately emerge bitter or better. Major life crises do not preclude anyone from achieving success."

Chapter 4

Success is on the Horizon

So, as narrated earlier, I got into high school after the crisis of losing my mother. I decided, "no way was this going to stop me; my mother is not here but I am".

I cannot remember exactly who said what or anything to me, but I knew that something in me was determined to carry on and I was determined to be the best that I could be. In fact, I was determined to fulfil that which my mother could not have fulfilled, now that she was gone. I purposed in my heart that I was going to do what mummy always wanted to do. I remember one day, going into the space underneath the cellar. Our house was on stilts and we had a huge space underneath which we called the cellar.

I was looking through some of my mother's things and I found a little book which documented some of the activities that she used to be involved in. There was a section written in shorthand writing and I remember that she talked about attending a secretarial school when she was in Kingston. Clearly, she had learned shorthand, a skill I never knew she possessed. I found some pictures, maybe of old friends. I rummaged through her belongings, thought about her and basked in her memory for a while. Those minutes or hours, however long the time might have been, reminded me that I had the opportunity to realise my dreams, but I could go a step further and bring her aspirations to fruition as well. My mind was set.

The trip to get to my high school every day was no mean feat. Every day I had to leave home very early in the morning; this could have been around 5am, to get to the bus stop on time. First, I had to conquer the four-mile walk to get there. If it happened to be raining, which on many occasions it was, I could not wear my school shoes from my home, because the road became very muddy and sticky. I had two choices: if it were a time when I was lucky enough to have another spare pair of older shoes that I could wear in the mud, I would wear it until I got to a certain point, where there was a bridge and running water.

I could use that water that was flowing underneath the bridge to wash my feet. Then I would don my school shoes. I would carefully hide the pair of old shoes somewhere around the area of the bridge and collect it on my way home in the evening. Hopefully, it would not have been too dark by the time I got there again in the evening. The other choice was to walk barefooted and wash my feet at the same point, before putting on my socks and school shoes.

Chapter 4

There was only one bus travelling that route at the time; that bus was called Hamlet and I think the driver was called Winston. I vaguely remember him - a quiet man. He was the owner of the bus and in my eyes, he was a wealthy man - he owned the bus! So that was the only bus that would ply that route to take us to a connecting town or point. We could either get off the bus at Summerfield or Chapelton to get another vehicle that would take us to school in Frankfield.

God help me if I missed the bus. Sometimes on my journey to the bus stop, I could hear the bus on its way because for some reason, the driver used to toot the horn - almost in a song, as the bus approached each major bus stop. This was, and probably still is common practice in Jamaica. You would hear the bus 'singing' and it was your warning signal.

The drivers knew that people from far and near would be hustling to get the bus and, as the only means of transport, in many cases, it would alert people to its imminent arrival at a bus stop. If you are lucky enough, or had set out on time, you would not miss the bus. There was one thing that often proved to be a saving grace and especially on certain mornings I would give thanks to the Lord and be grateful for the higglers. The market higglers are mostly women who would be travelling to the market to sell their produce. Since they had lots of goods like bunches of sugar cane; bags of oranges; bags of yams and other ground provisions like cocoa and dasheen and other things to be sold in the market, it took a while for the bus to leave that spot.

Hence, if I were running late, I would hope and hope that there would be a higgler at my particular bus stop. On certain mornings, I knew that Sister Clarice would be there, waiting with her load of produce to get on the bus. On occasions, I would be running and panting as I made my way. Sometimes, just managing to make it whilst they were still loading on the higgler's goods to the top of the bus. I would have made it 'just by the skin of my teeth', as we say in Jamaica. Looking back, it was almost an impossible task as there was no set timetable with the bus's arrival or departure time.

It was all a game of approximation, based on several factors, including the length of time that was spent at the previous bus stop. So, the bus may have arrived much earlier or later than expected.

Needless to say, it would be a jam-packed bus that I would be joining and in my tired state, there would not usually be a chance of having a seat on the bus - that would almost be a miracle! However, in all honesty, even if there was the opportunity to have a seat, I would not necessarily want to sit in my very crisp starched and nicely ironed cotton

Chapter 4

uniform. Sitting down meant running the risk of crushing my uniform.

The pleats were like the blade of a knife; they were very straight and stiff. We took much pride in our uniform and our general appearance. Later on, when polyester or other synthetic material became more common place, we started wearing gabardine, a type of synthetic cloth and though it still needed ironing, there was less pressure to maintain those very outstanding pleats and so we would be more inclined to sit whilst travelling on the bus on those times when we were fortunate enough to get a seat. But we were also very polite children, and we would not sit if there was any older person standing.

As a result, invariably, we would be standing all the way from boarding the bus, e.g., Wesleyan, in my case, to our point of disembarking, e.g., Summerfield. That journey could take anything up to an hour and a half on the very crowded bus; packed with people like sardines. Having got to Summerfield, there was another wait to get a minivan to go to Frankfield. This was not as difficult because there were many vans that plied that route.

On several occasions we got to school late and believe me, they were still administering corporal punishment to high school students then (1982) for late arrivals. If you arrived at school late either you would be locked out because the gate was closed or you would be allowed in but after a 'price' is paid at the gate. I understand there had to be a deterrent for arriving at school late, but it was so unfair to treat every child arriving at school as doing so out of nonchalance and lack of effort. Fear and trepidation would engulf me if I ever found myself being late. Unfortunately, there were about two occasions that I can recall, being in that situation.

A wooden cane or a leather strap would be used to administer the punishment – you would stand in front of the teacher with your arm outstretched and the cane / strap would be applied to the palm of your hand. I remember thinking how utterly unfair it was when I received that punishment, knowing the struggle and effort I made to even arrive at school. But such was the price that one had to pay; it was all a part of acquiring an education to become successful in life and lift myself out of my default position to a higher level in society.

Just thinking about the corporal punishment makes me shudder but that was the incentive to get us to arrive at school on time. Unfortunately, some of us did not have any control over the situation, as we were dependent on public transportation. In my case, very limited public transportation.

Whilst loading the produce of the higglers on to the bus was a saviour on some occasions, it was a factor that meant that the bus was often late to arrive

Chapter 4

at the destination where we disembarked. Loading the bus could take up to half hour, eating away at precious time to arrive at school.

Of course, this also rendered the bus top heavy, luckily, somehow balanced because there are so many people packed inside. However, the truth is that it was actually, a dangerous affair. Looking back, it is obvious that even the act of getting to school meant balancing pros and cons. As I stated earlier, the delay caused by loading the bus was on occasions, the 'God sent' opportunity that would allow us to catch the bus in the first place. Otherwise, we would have missed an entire day of school. I will never forget the day when I did miss the bus.

It had driven past my bus stop at Wesleyan before I could emerge from my parochial adjoining road for anyone to even notice that I was trying to get the bus. But even that little crisis presented an opportunity for me to embrace a new challenge in my quest for a better life. That day was the first and only time in my life that I have ever ridden on a motorbike. There was a well-known young man who lived in one of the neighbouring districts who owned a motorbike.

I recall him being popular for his entrepreneurial endeavours and probably because he was the only person in the area at the time who owned a motorbike and as far as I recall, he also owned a minivan. His name was Carl, but everyone called him 'Stamma', simply because he had a stutter. One thing that must be said is that Jamaicans are ingenious for assigning aliases to individuals. I reckon a whole book could be written on that subject. Many of the names would have been considered politically incorrect or outright offensive in another setting, but in Jamaica, it is just different and a hallmark of our honesty and forthrightness, I dare say.

Stamma turned up on his motorbike; I don't know where he was going but he took one look at me and said, "come on, get on the back of the bike". Oh, my goodness! There I was, this prim and proper little Christian girl getting on and straddling a motorbike behind this man – a complete stranger for all intents and purposes.

To compound the issue, he did not ride in a straight line along the road. Rather, he was dilly dallying and, to me, appeared to be all over the road. Of course, that is the way one would have to ride, to demonstrate mastery of the motorbike. I was holding on for dear life! I don't know but I must have held on to him during this necessary ordeal of kind act!

He managed to catch up with the bus. Of course, he would; the bus was much slower than his

Chapter 4

motorbike, especially, given how he rode and having his mission in mind to ensure that he got me on the bus. We rode to Blackwoods; there was Hamlet; it had stopped to pick up yet another load of produce for another higgler and there – Hey Presto! Stamma just said, "there's your bus". I cannot recall if I ever spoke to Stamma again and I wonder whether he recalled this kind act, but I remember it very well to this very day. I know I would have said thank you on the day but acts like these warrant special thanks. I'm uncertain whether he is still alive. Whether or not, I'd like to say, "Thanks again, Stamma!"

We may have never had the opportunity to talk about that encounter and experience. He was just not somebody that I knew to talk to on a personal level, though he was well known in the area and showed up for me when I really needed him. He was certainly my angel or shall we say, my knight on motor bike on the day!

So, once we got to school, it was the next phase of a long arduous day. However, I enjoyed school and being very proud to have made it to high school, I was invested in giving it my best shot. I excelled, even with a significant portion of my study time being the period during my bus rides in the evening on the way home. Things did start changing as we progressed through high school; we started having access to other vehicles plying the route.

CAN WOMEN HAVE IT ALL?

After Hamlet was no more, we had access to a number of mini vans and larger ones that we called 'coasters'. I remember there was one that was driven by 'Teacher' and then there was one that was driven by 'Costi' – both names are unique Jamaican aliases, given to these men for 'whatever' reasons.

Missing these vehicles, meant a small chance of getting another vehicle but always a very slim chance and highly uncertain. Later, Costi's van started plying the route from Wesleyan / Thompson Town directly to Frankfield. That was a major improvement for the prospects of getting to school with much less hassle and in good time. Unfortunately, it still meant trekking the four-mile journey on my parochial path to get to a suitable pick-up point on the main road.

In the evenings, the bus to get back home was called Suzette. Suzette was famous and the drivers of the Suzette buses were young men who were very popular with the female students. Suzette Transport comprised a fleet of buses - all called Suzette (but perhaps with secondary names) which I did not notice at the time.

The business was owned by a family with many sons - I remember Junior and Jimmy. Jimmy was pleasant; he knew me as the girl who is always studying on the bus. I recall being told that Suzette was the name of the family's only daughter.

Chapter 4

However, we never saw her. One ubiquitous female associated with Suzette Transport was the indomitable conductress on the bus - a lady called Betty.

Betty was a no-nonsense woman! Even though every evening the bus would be packed like sardines with school children, no one could evade Betty by not paying the bus fare. Some children did try but Betty seemed to know every one of us and where each one was due to get off the bus. I look back in wonderment at her skills and ingenuity.

It is just amazing how us human beings can adapt and make the best of situations in the most challenging of circumstances. She was known to be fierce, but she was loved. There was a gentleness about her, despite the harsh exterior. I would say she had a motherly touch. To this day, I remember exactly what she looks like and can visualise Betty collecting the fares on the extremely crowded Suzette Bus. The story concerning the higglers and their produce rang true as well for Suzette as it did for Hamlet. A significant amount of time was spent in the evenings loading on the higglers' goods for the market.

Although we would be parked up at places for aeons, because these women were not just travelling to local markets but to the much bigger markets in Kingston, where they would spend days selling their produce. As you can imagine, they had to carry enough goods to make it worth their while and believe me, they did! Our Suzette bus made a round trip from Kingston to the Country (Spaulding) every day. I wish I had photos of this bus when it was loaded! It is heart stopping to even consider now. Moreover, Suzette has a special place in my heart as the place where I did most of my studying during my high school career. I had simply worked out that it was the only way for me to survive high school successfully.

There simply was not enough time to study when I arrived home each day. However, far from being a nice cosy and quiet study area, the bus was alive and packed with activities all the time. The physical jolting, bobbing and twisting of the roller coaster ride on the bus was another matter.

The roads were very narrow; sometimes physically over precipices - just a tiny, narrow road and precipice on either side. Sometimes, it would be a tiny, precarious bridge over a swelling river, especially when it rained. To compound the matter, the drivers did not navigate these little roads slowly.

They would continue at great speed, tooting the horn in songs as the bus is driven over these undulating and precarious roads. It must be said, however, that the drivers must have been extremely skilful. Nonetheless, I am sure it was nothing short

Chapter 4

of a miracle, how we survived those daily journeys. Travelling on these vehicles was also a time of hilarity and joy for most of the school children and, even for me, it was an opportunity for sharing and time to have some fun with friends. Most of the children had different circumstances to me. Their journey home was much shorter – the bus/vehicle even stopping just outside of their front doors and they would have had the luxury of electricity to ensure good lighting to aid their study and revision.

For me and a few others, the extended length of our bus journey meant that I travelled further to Thompson Town. After I disembarked from the bus, I would walk home for about five miles – an additional mile in the evenings. On arriving home, I was tired and by this time it was invariably dark.

The kerosene lamp would not provide the light that I needed to study. Furthermore, where would I even sit down to study? There was one bedroom accommodating my other three siblings and later, when my stepmother's children arrived, we had even less space. Still, I was determined that those circumstances would not stop me from getting top grades at school.

I was undoubtedly learning the art of making use of even small opportunities and developing my time management skills. Even if I was unaware of the far-reaching nature of these lessons at the time, the value of such attributes to achieving success has become increasingly evident. So many individuals in my community were looking up to me.

They were expecting me to do commendable things, which meant I was expected to conduct myself with utmost care. I remember one evening as I was walking home in the twilight, there were footsteps behind me. There was a young man following me; he said something about wanting to have a relationship.

Of course, I flatly refused but this guy would appear on several evenings on my way home. I was adamant that this would never happen. I do not think he ever intended to hurt me but it's somewhat chilling thinking about it now. I believe God protected me from the eventualities that could have resulted from such scenarios. He soon got the message and stopped bothering me. I remember his name and who he is. Somehow, I was not afraid. On another late evening, I had another unforgettable experience. It was very late and dark, and it had rained.

I remember walking in the dark, but this was not usually a problem because I was accustomed to the road. I knew the road even though many areas were just winding tiny tracks with what we call 'brockway' on either side. Due to the inclement weather pattern, the land would recede and often

Chapter 4

there would be bits of the earth tearing away gradually.

On this particular night as I negotiated one of those precarious little paths, located in a ravine, as it were, between Gloucester and Reid Piece, shortly after leaving the Drummond's shop, I turned off the longer route to take my usual short cut, in order to get home in a much shorter time. I was walking along confidently, when, what we call a 'winky' or a 'Peeney Waally' (firefly) just shone its unusually bright light in front of me.

Each time I think about this incident, my heart skips a beat and I just thank God for His protection. I was on the brink of one of these 'Brockway' and would have stepped off the path into a precipice, had the firefly not shone its light. I think a new area of land had receded and broken off, changing the familiar layout of the path. Had I taken another step, I would have, undoubtedly been significantly hurt.

I have often joked that I was saved by the 'Peeny Waally' but deep down, I know it was the divine work of God that saved me from sure danger – just like He promised He would do in Psalm 91. That Psalm that I had read to my mum on numerous occasions. Going to high school meant that I was now going to school five days per week, versus the four-day week in primary school.

CAN WOMEN HAVE IT ALL?

The fact is that when I was at school on a Friday, my siblings were not. They were still helping to get the produce ready for the market on Saturday. In all fairness my siblings had more experience of digging yams, chopping bananas and sugar cane then I had, because I escaped that whilst being at school.

That was one of the reasons why I vowed to help my siblings and to make sure that when I succeeded, they would as well. I have done my best to remain true to such a promise and those resolutions and gestures contribute to the very close relationship that we share to this day.

The other thing that I was told, which I did not quite realise, was that on many mornings after I had left for school, nobody could have breakfast, except something directly obtained from the land, e.g., oranges. Fortunately, there was a good amount of produce around so one could have a fruit and find something to eat. But the point is that there was no money left for anything else after my father gave me whatever little money was in the house for bus fare and to get lunch at school.

When the school week was finished, Saturday was washday and washing was not about putting clothes in the washing machine. To begin with, there was no electricity. We had to collect our clothes, take them to the river and half or three quarters of the day was spent washing on a Saturday. After

Chapter 4

washing, we would go to look for food, what we used to call 'feeding' for the pigs that we reared. This would entail pulling grass and other appropriate plants with our hands. There are certain types of grass and watercress type grass (watergrass) that we would look for. We became very efficient at spotting these plants but, the truth remains that it was a very tedious job, especially when one is tired after washing large amounts of clothes. By the time, we had finished that task, the clothes that we had spread out on the hot river stones were dry.

It was a time of pleasure and playing for some children who took the time after to go and have a swim and play in the water but that was not what I did. I felt I could not spare the time to play and learn to swim as I had to get back home.

I needed to study and as I was a Sunday School teacher, so also needed to prepare my lesson as well as prepare for leading the Youth Ministries Meetings on Sunday evenings. The outcome is that, though I grew up in that district, surrounded by water, I never learnt to swim. It is indeed, as an adult that I took swimming lessons. In retrospect, I think I would have done this differently. Knowing what I know now, I would have made some time to play and engage the child in me. Those precious times can never be recovered.

Minister McKenzie who we affectionately referred to as 'Minis' was my mentor in church and when I was around him I spoke no patois but 'proper' English. I loved this, it was not an issue for me. Then Minister McKenzie went off to Teacher's College. He would write lovely long letters to the church whilst he was away and Sister Carol would stand in front of the church in the pulpit and read them to the congregation.

I enjoyed doing that; it reminded me of the Apostle Paul and his letters to the church in the New Testament. I wish I had copies of those letters but even if I had requested and obtained permission to do so, there were no facilities to copy them. It would have been nice to see those letters now; he is a lengthy writer, a man of many words and I recall those letters were really encouraging.

We would really look forward to receiving his letters, as a church. I am very grateful today to Minis; I owe so much to him. We never actually sat down and had a good talk to reminisce about those times. He has lived up to his message of continuous personal, professional, and spiritual development and has, himself, done very well. He is now Dr Canute Livingstone McKenzie and Bishop of that group of churches that we were part of growing up. I salute my biggest adolescent mentor. Thanks a million for mentoring me.

Chapter 4

There is overwhelming evidence to show that mentoring is a key factor in shaping individuals for success.

Furthermore, educating and mentoring girls go a long way to uplifting not just the individual but the world at large. For me mentorship allowed for practical advice, encouragement and support. To learn from the experience of my mentors, allowing me to develop not just academically but socially and spiritually which in turn massively boosted my confidence and empowered me to make decisions, even in tough times.

"Having hope and a positive mindset will always propel you to grasping success. Sometimes it is the unlikeliest feature that provides a lifeline when you need it."

Chapter 5

Crisis Take 2 – Coping in a Blended Family

(Building success despite the disadvantages of a blended family)

We were elated! Finally, we would have a 'mother', somebody, an adult woman who had come to live with us. Most people would not consider the scenario of an adult female moving into a family with four young children without a mother, a crisis. However, the event of our stepmother coming to live with us was on some level, exactly that. If for nothing else, from the perspective of having to embrace change.

Fortunately, everything started off well. She seemed very caring. The novelty of having a mother figure in the home was appreciated and embraced. Our stepmother told us many rather fascinating stories about her life. We genuinely enjoyed her stories and started bonding with her. She seemed very excited about having my father as a partner. In fact, from what she told us, it was a dream come true for her and she may have been the envy of a few other women.

Apparently, there had been mutual attraction between her and daddy way back in the past, but their circumstances did not allow for a relationship at the time. They had both enjoyed their separate lives and were now at this point in history. A point that she seemed willing and rearing to cherish.

I believe that she cared for us; even if it was transient. For us, anything devoid of overt abuse would have been considered good at that point. We were by nature, 'low maintenance' children and genuinely just needed some semblance of love and motherly care, having lived without a mother for a considerable amount of time. The primary benefit was that she assisted us with organising ourselves so we could get more out of our days and plan better for future activities.

For example, ensuring that we did not run out of water and firewood and that the animals were fed in a timelier manner. Also, that our evening meals were better planned and prepared at an earlier time. This did not mean any less work for us, just a difference in strategy and execution. In fact, on some occasions, we felt it was unnecessary to do some of the chores, e.g., getting firewood and water when there was plenty at home.

Her argument was that we should always have more than we need – "prepare for rainy day" she would say. The real test of our relationship came when daddy went abroad to his farm work job which he did yearly. This was going to be the first

Chapter 5

time, being left on our own with somebody new and different. So here we were for the first time on our own with this new but somewhat intriguing lady. To be fair, the first year went quite well, from my recollection. We coped; she provided an adult presence and guidance and looked after us as needed. In turn, we worked with her - the cows were looked after, she was impressive with this, I must say, the donkey was fed, the pigs were fed and the farming crops were harvested and prepared for sale in the market.

We predominantly sold the produce to higglers but on occasions, she would go to the market to sell the produce herself. Her gift of bringing order and structure to our lives and having that responsible adult as part of our lives was, perhaps, her greatest asset to us and we appreciated and benefitted from this for the most part. This arrangement carried on for a while without any major conflict.

Unfortunately, cracks started appearing in our relationship. For some unknown reason, at least to me, our stepmother saw me as some sort of a threat and started to treat me differently. I am not sure why, but she did refer to me as my father's 'spoilt child' – meaning he treated me specially. My experience was that she found ways and means of putting a wedge in the relationship between me and my father. As if this was not enough, the environment she created, fostered some division between me and my siblings. Words cannot explain how heartrending this was! Here we were, having lost our mother; through no fault of her own she had died at the tender age of 31 years. I had stepped in and assumed the maternal responsibility and had been the one that my siblings looked up to, but all this was now under threat.

This persisted and there were occasions when we exchanged, shall we say, "very strong words". Even at this time I was very independent and there was no way I was about to roll over and allow anybody to come into our home and, in my view, try to disrupt our family. Moreover, I was articulate and confident enough to use this tool to my advantage. Hence, when she tried to do anything that to me was unbecoming, I would tell her how I felt about her actions.

Rest assured that these words, on my part, were all exchanged in 'proper English', never in Patois, with particular emphasis on the words that I felt needed to be enunciated and highlighted. This in itself would have made her even more irate and I was accused of "using big words" on her.

The ability to express one's feelings confidently and fluently is often viewed as threatening and sometimes labelled as 'aggression'. Such an ability, somehow, has the effect of making the other person appear and feel inferior if they feel they are not able

Chapter 5

to match you in the discourse. For me it was a victory because, not only had I not used derogatory language or opted for expletives and conducted myself as what we term in Jamaica "a ghetto gal" but I had articulated my points and expressed my feelings in an intelligent and respectable way.

That was the weapon I had and that was what I used! That way she was left in no doubt about how I felt about her actions. But you guessed it, this did not go down very well. Unfortunately, it appeared to fuel more vicious attacks on me. I hasten to clarify that these were never physical. But if I had not known before those experiences that our common playground adage, "sticks and stones may break my bones, but words can do me no harm" is totally false and unfounded. I learnt then that the hurt caused by malicious words is indeed very painful and can inflict incredibly deep wounds which may take years to heal.

On the auspicious occasion of my 18th birthday, my father was away in America, so I decided to write him a letter expressing and outlining what turning 18 meant for me. On his return home, my stepmother decided that she would read my letter/s that I had written to my father. She took offense to the content of this letter and started another war with me, based on the content of the letter. I had in good innocent faith written a letter to my father outlining the fact and my gratitude and realisation that I had become an adult and that I could now legally make my own decisions and such the like - out of pure innocence reminiscing about where we had come from and how time had passed and now his little girl had become an adult.

Unfortunately, she chose to interpret this as me being rude and even though this was, initially of no offence to my father, she planted the idea in his mind that I was being rude and out of place to have sent him such a letter.

She told him how I was thinking that I'm an adult and was being disrespectful to have sent such a letter to him. Bearing in mind, that my father was of significantly limited literary skills, he bought into my stepmother's interpretation of the letter and for a while, also appeared to subscribe to her notions about the contents. This was exactly what my stepmother wanted. The "rude 18th birthday letter" scenario caused significant conflict and untold stressful dynamics in our family.

It's worth noting that the letter would have initially been read to daddy by a close friend whilst he was in America as he was unable to read it for himself. He perhaps felt that his friend would have been too polite to say anything untoward, but daddy should know that was not characteristic of a Jamaican and his friend would have expressed concern if he felt that his daughter was being rude in

Chapter 5

her letter to her father. Things continued to go downhill and to make matters worse, her three children also moved in to live with us later. The problem here was not merely the significantly limited space for accommodation but it was the struggles and protracted battle of cohabitating with individuals with totally different values, mindsets and goals.

"But" I hear you ask, "How many more children, how many more individuals can live in this two-bedroom house? I suspect I could have been writing a jolly tale about how we all cohabitated and had fun despite the spatial challenges, however, unfortunately, that was not how the story went.

Nevertheless, we were forgiving children and these were children of our stepmother, so despite everything, we did our best to foster a smooth assimilation. Initially, we would spend evenings talking and sharing jokes and learning new things about each other's lifestyles.

It was all novel to us and some of the things that they had experienced as children, we had never experienced. So, we did enjoy the evening stories which, undoubtedly fostered opportunities to learn about and understand each other. I remember them telling us about somebody who used to watch television which we did not have at that time and this person would refer to the television as "T-H-E" instead of TV. So, the person would say, "I'm going up to such and such a person's house to watch some T-H-E".

This was a simple and otherwise insignificant anecdote, but for some reason, we found the account hilarious at the time and it became a unique and private joke between us. To this day, if I say to my sisters, "I am going to watch some T-H-E, we will each burst out laughing! Unfortunately, but not surprisingly, the children sided with their mother and the family dynamics got even worse. One thing that was noticeable and quite sad, was that no longer was it second nature for all concerned to keep our little two-bedroom house 'spick-and-span' and the floors shining like silver sparked polished red wood.

Growing up, we had no problem polishing and shining the floor using the genie floor polish. It was our pride and joy to see the floor shine in its glory. Unfortunately, our new occupants were not as enthusiastic to participate in these chores and soon we started resenting the fact that they were sharing the house but were not keen to participate in cleaning and taking care of it.

To us, this was a bizarre behaviour that was beyond our understanding and it did become a source of further problems. In addition, the washing on Saturdays had taken on a completely different

Chapter 5

ethos. Whereas it was previously just part of our weekly routine, our new occupants also seemed to find it extremely difficult and were also reticent at participating in this task. All the chores which were second nature to us previously and were shared amongst ourselves without any question, now became hard tasks with everybody unwilling to participate simply because there was no longer a feeling of a united and shared workload.

Our once laissez-faire home environment had become extremely stressful. Things had changed; what a difference a stepmother made! Needless to say, the repercussions of losing our mother became more tangible and the pain was more palpable. It was the pain of young children in a crisis that needed to be managed so it did not cause lasting damage. How do you negotiate that?

Believe it or not, we never complained to our father and he never seemed to realise the magnitude of all that was going on. The situation was compounded by the fact that for many months of the year he was not around because he left at certain times of the year to go to America on his farm work.

This was the only significantly lucrative employment that he had to generate enough money to build a house so that we could move from the two-bedroom house that we were living in. Also, to move to an area where there was potable running water, a road instead of a track and electricity. Having said that, it is worth noting that our status in the district, had become a bit more elevated as by this time daddy had bought a portable generator to provide electricity.

I still remember the name of it: 'Honda EM500 Portable Generator' – oh my goodness! On some nights, the generator would be turned on, which meant that we would have electricity!

The TV would be plugged in but all that was visible, was predominantly 'white grains' with opaque similitudes of people. Despite this, significant numbers of people would flock to our house because of the bright light and the music playing. People would be huddled together to glare at the television even though the pictures were essentially non-existent; incapable to make any sense of them. In retrospect, this was all hilarious, but we enjoyed it, nonetheless.

Those were some of the benefits that we enjoyed from daddy travelling yearly to America. This was in lieu of him not always being there physically. One could argue that the price was high but I don't know whether daddy would have made much difference, even if he was always around. He was such a docile person; so calm, he never made anything a problem. Although this was good in one sense, in my opinion, it has proven to be a

Chapter 5

problematic trait at times but has remained an enduring characteristic of daddy, even to this day. Unfortunately, the same could not be said of my step-mother; it appears she constantly tried to manipulate circumstances and individuals when she could.

It is sad that as humans, we may allow negative emotions such as jealousy, to cloud our vision and ruin our perspectives. I wish my stepsister had had conversations with me and expressed how she felt about her own life and upbringing and the situation that we had found ourselves in. There could have been some deep and meaningful conversations between us. However, instead of talking to me, and sharing thoughts as two young women, she chose to demonstrate pure hate.

Later, as an adult, she wrote me a letter, telling me how spoilt I was (no need to guess where those words originated from) and expressing pure venom and dislike for me. I am still trying to fathom the concept of me being spoilt. Far from being wrapped in cotton wool and being pampered, I had no shortage of untold harsh realities. The most I am able to say on this is that I think God's favour on one's life may be misinterpreted by many.

When one is generally loved and respected in any environment, it is bound to be viewed unfavorably by some. This is an important life principle for understanding and achieving success. It baffles me how someone may choose to hate another person just because the individual is perceived to be liked more.

For me, it was even more baffling when you have tried, when you shared your personal space with someone and tried to accommodate them, when you have tried to make them feel welcome, but just for being you, somebody hates you.

This has prompted extensive introspection on my part; however, I am still unable to work out how I might have acted differently at the time to avoid the animosity. I certainly was not about to compromise my ambitions and aspirations. My siblings do not think for one second that I was one to be boastful or vindictive, so I am still at a loss but take comfort that there is evidence that I am not just being conceited.

Chapter 5

"Always be resourceful and use whatever skill or tool you possess or can access in a crisis. This is a biblical principle worth noting and embracing, e.g., Moses and his rod and Sampson and the strength of his 'bare hands'.

We will never please everyone in life; there will always be someone who does not agree with your point of view or simply does not like you. Succeed anyway! Moreover, there is good in the worst of us and some bad in the best of us."

Chapter 6

Success achieved - I'm outta here!

High school is now finished and my dream to attend nursing school to train to become a nurse has been realised. It has been a tough ride. My stepmother had stated clearly that I would not be going anywhere because my father simply did not have the money to fund my nursing school education. This was even told to me by individuals in the district who were not family members.

A personal friend thought she needed to put me straight; one day she said to me: "Carol, I know you are planning to go to nursing school, but your stepmother has said it won't happen" - paraphrasing. She said (patois): "you can stay dere plan to go a nursing school. Pason (my father) need fi build him house before he can send her to any nursing school".

I am not sure whether my friend just wanted to make me aware of what was being said or whether her intention was also to 'put me in my place' regarding my big dream. Whatever the intention, hearing this from someone outside of our home meant to me that these things were being discussed with 'strangers' outside of our household and in a negative way.

Chapter 6

That information only fueled my tenacity and from that moment I was even more determined than ever to get into nursing school. My mindset then was like a dog with a good bone! I would pray again and again with dogged determination and I worked my hardest to get the grades I needed. I sought and accessed every bit of information and help that I could get from my limited resources at the time – mainly my school library and my teachers - to realise this goal.

On one occasion my stepmother had an appointment in Kingston, and I decided I would get on the bus with her so that I could find the nursing school in Kingston and that's exactly what I did. On the morning she was scheduled to go into Kingston, I got dressed, walked to the bus stop and got on the bus with her. I cannot recall whether I had money to pay my bus fare but, maybe that was of less importance to me.

In the end, she accompanied me to the nursing school in Mona, after her appointment. I believe this was divine intervention but even if one wants to argue that she simply became as curious as I was; we both got to see the nursing school I desired to attend - University Hospital of the West Indies (UHWI) School of Nursing. Most importantly, that day, I got to speak to the Admissions Officer and got the facts that I really needed. (Remember, I did not have access to a telephone or the internet at that time as we do now).

On that day I learnt some important and truly liberating facts. I learnt that I would NOT be required to pay a fee to attend nursing school. Once I secure the exam grades I needed and passed the nursing school's entrance requirements which included an interview and writing an essay, I would be admitted. That was music to my ears and that confirmed for me, that I would be going to nursing school, come hell or high water! Of course, there was no evidence that this was not in God's will for my life, so I was going to do my level best to make this happen.

Once I knew where the nursing school was, there would be no problem with me returning for the number of times that I needed to return there. Whether it was to sit the entrance examination, for the interview or whatever else. I just needed to know where I was heading, and I had got that out of the way. It is important to appreciate that times were slightly different then, certainly there was no access to the internet. Access to transportation and information at the best of times in my country, at that time, was a challenge.

Never mind for a country girl like me whose home had no routine access to electricity and who

Chapter 6

was not coming from a place with proper roads to access the limited transportation system.

For me, the best way was to physically get to the nursing school, it was the best way I knew to get the information I needed once and for all. Of course, had my stepmother not had an appointment in Kingston, I would have found another way but what an opportunity that was! Even if she was not speaking to me when we boarded the bus that day, she was, by the time the day's journey ended. In fact, during her appointment we came across some friends and she was, nothing short of boasting, that her stepdaughter would be going to nursing school and that she was helping me.

Whether this was a case of making her 'look good' in their eyes or an "if you can't beat them, join them" scenario, I was not concerned, as long as I achieved the outcome of getting to that nursing school that day. Thank God, that was realised. It was a case of seeing an opportunity, grasping it, and achieving. A minor victory in the eyes of some but a major one for me that day, which would have significant implications for the rest of my life!

So, the day arrived when I left my wonderful, familiar and safe little district - Windsor for the big city of Kingston. I was finally going to nursing school! I packed my suitcase. I put on my cute little yellow skirt and blouse - what I called my 'yellow suit'. It was just a pale yellow polyester skirt and a cotton blouse with a similar hue that daddy had brought back for me from one of his American trips.

The two went very well together and I still remember what I looked like with my perfect figure (at least to me!), all dressed up, ready with my little suitcase. I remember the morning; it was a Sunday morning; my siblings came out with me to the top of the path that led from our house - we refer to that area as "up a gate". 'Up a gate' was an established outdoor congregational point for the district. I am not sure if it had a true central geographical position, but much could be viewed from that point. Some called that little geographical area within Windsor, with all the houses, the church and the main shop in the district - Colorado.

'Up a gate' was the centre of Colorado. It was a lovely flat terrain, though it was essentially at the top of an incline. The area was void of a central imposing structure, such as a tree, hence, the sun always seemed to shine on that spot, making it bright and inviting as a central congregational and viewing area.

Our house was located at the bottom of the incline from this spot. The path to our house was lined on either side with hibiscus plants which, from my recollection, were in various stages of bloom throughout the year. As children, we would often

Chapter 6

grab a flower in full bloom as we passed by – maybe to place in our hair or just to admire it. Or picked a partially bloomed flower with its partly closed petals, to use as a kind of a musical instrument, like a recorder. When we blew into the half-closed flower, the force of the air from our breath, partly escaping between the compacted petals would cause a musical sound and we would simulate songs or just make random blowing musical sounds whilst blowing into it.

Directly across and levelling with the central area of 'up a gate', was another house (The Pennants), further eastward was another house (The Whites) and then Westward was our indomitable church building - not auspicious but a building with an air of authority and reverence. If one's eyes were raised, his or her line of vision would be drawn to the hills nearby – Johncrow hill at one end and the infamous "Manbump" hill about half a mile away; so, named for its notoriously steep incline – it was no easy feat negotiating that hill after a shower of rain.

Only those who have experienced being stuck in the mud with the dilemma of where next to place the other foot can truly appreciate the reality of this hill. This area was also somewhat of a phone as one could call, i.e., shout someone's name from a distance. There, in that spot, my family congregated and waved me goodbye. I went off with my suitcase.

Alone but happy. I got the bus after walking the 4 miles to the bus stop and after a few bus changes and a journey of about 3 hours, arrived at the nurses' home or "nurses' residence" as we referred to it - it sounded better, and it allowed for a lesser chance of mistaking our residence for a 'nursing' (rather than nurses') home. So, this was the Nurses' Residence of the University Hospital of the West Indies School of Nursing.

I later learned this place of residence was fondly called 'the Bastille Towers'. On arrival, I realised I was one of a kind! Yes, this time not in reference to the fact that I am uniquely created and purposed by God but one of a kind in the sense that I was the only one who arrived at the UHWI Nurses' Residence on my own. Not to mention, having arrived on the bus with a suitcase. Even though this was 1988, all my other student nurse colleagues had arrived with a parent or other relative/s in a car that had dropped them off at the reception area of the nursing school / residence.

As I turned up with my suitcase, having arrived in a bus which, fortunately dropped me off at the entrance of the UHWI hospital, hence, a short walk on a nicely paved road to the Nurses' Residence which is located on the hospital grounds, I was checked in by Sister Jarret – the formidable, no nonsense Sister in charge of the Nurses' Residence. She was to become an integral part of all our lives

Chapter 6

for the next few years. I went upstairs and embraced the reality, to my great delight, that I would have a room of my own, my own room A12 on the third floor of the A block.

I settled into my room and packed my things away. I could not believe it – I would have a room all to myself for the foreseeable future. Luxury! We had a communal bathroom, but it was large and well laid out with compartmental shower units and toilets – I could deal with that. It was a significant improvement from the zinc and bamboo extension that was adjoined to our home in Windsor and had running water where a shower could be taken with water from the rising main as against being thrown over one's body with a smaller container from a plastic or metal bath tub / pan. Moreover, there was the option to have a warm shower without the need to first boil the water over a wooden fire!

I also learnt during this time that we would be provided with three meals a day, seven days a week, free of cost AND here was the bonus – we would be given a STIPEND (bursary) every month – imagine that! I did not realise any of this before but, boy, was I made up. This was absolute bliss! Just imagine if I had listened to the narrative that my father was not able to afford to send me to nursing school? I would probably still be stuck in Windsor until this day, thinking that I am trapped and have no means of escaping. Never allow anyone, to talk you out of your dreams. There is always a way if you desire it enough!

The journey had only just started. The course went very well but of course there were challenges. However, I completed my three-year nurse training program and gained the qualification of becoming a registered general nurse (RGN) in 1991. It was shortly after our arrival at nursing school, in the same year, 1988, that Jamaica was hit by the famous Hurricane Gilbert. I remember us looking through the large windows of the secured nurses' residence, all of us experiencing a hurricane for the very first time; watching Gilbert wreaking havoc as it tossed branches, trees and the rooves of houses in the wind, like mere toys.

The trail and magnitude of the destruction it left behind was to be lamented and remembered for years to come. The effects of the hurricane signaled our first major challenges at Nursing School. Even as first year student nurses we did not escape being part of the workforce that manned the wards during this time, but we embraced the challenge with its novelties and weathered that 'stormy' period, even with all its difficulties. My outlook was that, at least we had three meals a day because the hospital was responsible for looking after us whilst we helped to care for the patients and dealt with the disaster and health care challenges that occurred because of the hurricane. Many suffered greatly and lost the ability

Chapter 6

to meet one of mankind's basic needs of providing food for themselves and their families.

After completing my three-year nursing course in 1991, I worked for a year as a registered nurse and then went on to do my midwifery training. This required another year of full-time training to become a qualified midwife. In those days, a nurse did not do midwifery simply because s/he wanted to become a midwife to deliver babies; rather, it was done as a matter of course, if you wanted to progress your nursing career, regardless of the area you wanted to specialise in.

I think it is the autonomy that midwifery training and practice allows for; it was another level, in addition to our three years of general nursing education, that was required to work in a leadership role. It goes without saying, though that some individuals chose this path as their vocation. Of course, Carol wanted to progress her career, so she did midwifery; not knowing where it might take her. I enjoyed the course thoroughly and was rewarded with two leadership prizes at the end of it. I worked as a midwife for two years before I emigrated abroad to work in the Cayman Islands.

It would be remiss of me to talk about Nursing and Midwifery schools and not talk about my very influential nursing and midwifery tutors. Most of them were trained in the United Kingdom. They were an army of outstanding, well balanced, and refined individuals. They were amazing and very inspirational; we aspired to be like them, often emulating their unique characters, even if done in joke and jest. We had tutors like Mrs Scarlett, she was ever so charming; Mrs Adair - just the way she walks is unforgettable; not to mention Miss Estein who became one of our batch tutors.

This woman was in a class of her own - feisty was a euphemism to describe her. With her glasses perched at the tip of her nose, she would give us classic little lectures - well dictated and articulated with emphasis. Then she would look down at us over the rim of the glasses and at the end of it, lifted her head in the air with one swift act of extension and strut away with her classic gait of a well poised and proportioned woman, bursting with confidence. You just needed to see her to believe it! It is those women who left an indelible impression on my mind, and I believe, on the minds of many others.

Then there were others like Mrs Norma Woodham, the head of the nursing school. Now she was a case in point. Many of her lectures were spent telling us about her time in England and about her beloved family. She taught sociology, so maybe that can be forgiven. Sister Richie, Head of Midwifery took a more impersonal approach, though she was one of my 'warmest' tutors. She did not talk about family but was a fount of midwifery knowledge and

Chapter 6

skills. With her authoritative but endearing demeanor, she can never be forgotten. These women had a lot of influence on us, certainly on me and I pledged that one day I would go to the UK - the 'mother country' where these amazing and sterling women were trained, to experience what they experienced, so that I could be somehow, even in part, like they were.

In my mind, they modelled excellence and that was what I aimed for; they modelled success and that was what I aspired to. I was going to go wherever it took me to be able to acquire their level of expertise but also to share their stories and the experiences that shaped them to become who they were. Church remained a big part of my life and very high on my agenda. That was always going to continue because herein was something integral to my being, that I was a part of and that I would never give up under any circumstances.

Being a part of my church family and activities is demonstrative of my relationship with God; my heavenly father and would always be paramount to me achieving success and becoming who I really need to be. So, I continued attending church with my fellow Christian batch mates. I soon found Millicent Anderson, an exemplary nurse who was then a student nurse about two years my senior. Millicent adopted me as her little sister, though even now she often refers to me as her daughter (although she is only a few years older than I am). I started attending the church that she was a member of then - Bethel United Church of Jesus Christ, Apostolic, located at 20 South Camp Road in Kingston. Bethel was perfect in so many ways. Under the leadership of Bishop Ira D. Thompson, the church catered to my spiritual needs whilst I pursued my academic ambitions. 'South Camp' as the church is often affectionately referred to is still very dear to my heart and will always be.

I did not become very involved in church at South Camp as I was in my church in Windsor. I attended regularly, although it was a challenge negotiating the church services' schedule with that of my nursing duty rota. Looking back, however, I acknowledge that my real challenge started after I met Alex (pseudonym). He was the perfect gentleman. Perfect, because he met the first criteria of being a Christian who seemed to love the Lord as much as I did.

Perfect because his physical attributes plumb aligned with what I had in mind, in terms of physical criteria for a husband. Furthermore, he treated me like a princess and who would not be attracted to such chivalry and endorsement. Our friendship became courtship and the relationship lasted for about five years. For several reasons, our courtship did not culminate in a marriage as I had dreamt it would.

Chapter 6

Needless to say, I learnt a few lessons and my character was developed in another dimension. This was my first experience of truly being in love and now, I had lost that – Crisis? My hopes were severely dashed. Even now I can remember standing up that evening and watching him walk away when I said, "No" after realising and acknowledging 'red flags' in the relationship that would significantly compromise who I truly was.

Knowing that my heart was being shattered into a million pieces but still deciding on that course of action was perhaps my biggest personal test about an issue that could thwart the course I was on. I had lowered my standards to some extent but there was a line that I would not cross and I still had a chance to save me.

So, I stood and watched the love of my life walk away. I needed the love and comfort of my friends, especially the selfless and caring Millicent. I also needed help from my pastor and support from another very effective female leader in the church, but I healed. It took some time but yet another crisis was managed, and I needed to move on. Nursing school had given me the career I dreamt of at the time and ALMOST a marriage.

"Whatever you need to achieve success is already present; however, we are often required to implement ingenious ways to realise the solutions.

Sometimes you have to walk away; you must know when!"

Chapter 7

The Ultimate Land of Success

(England - the 'mother country')

So, I dreamt of going to the mother country. I have seen my tutors and admired their competencies and their general deportment – impeccable from where I stood! I had also seen nurses who came across to Jamaica from England - they were confident, fun loving and warmly embraced their profession.

They enjoyed Jamaica but they were different too… For the first time I saw people with blonde hair. It looked strange to me and I could not get my head around having that colour hair, especially as it seemed it was preferable to dark hair.

The Caucasian nurses who had dark hair just looked more 'natural' to me. Growing up in rural Jamaica, the only concept of a white person was from having a doll. I cannot recall whether I had seen a doll with blonde hair as a child but if I had, that would have been my only previous exposure to blonde hair. I laugh at myself now, knowing what we all know to be the concept of a blonde individual being more beautiful. More striking, was to later learn that some individuals took this concept even further, postulating the Aryan race's superiority.

The nurses who visited the UHWI from England were very friendly, and I got to know some of them. There was one nurse, in particular – Suzan, who spent some time working with me on one of the wards. Naturally, we got talking, as you do. She told me what it was like to work as a nurse in the UK and she gave me the information for the then United Council for Nursing, Midwifery and Health Visiting (UKCC), now the Nursing and Midwifery Council (NMC) and told me how to get registered with this body.

She explained that that was the registration and regulation body for nurses and midwives and further explained that one must be registered with this organisation in order to work as a nurse in the UK. Since Jamaica used to be a British colony, we had reciprocity with Britain and vice versa. Hence, for them to work in Jamaica as nurses, they did not need any additional training and the same applied for me if I wanted to work in the UK. I just needed to get registered with the UKCC.

Once that was done, I would need to find a job in the UK, then I would be able to work as a nurse in the UK via a work permit. That absolutely excited me and gave me confidence, so I started exploring the process to realise another deeply held ambition.

Chapter 7

However, I decided to put the UKCC's registration on hold and instead went to work in the Cayman Islands for a while. After two years of working in the Cayman Islands, during which time I got very much more exposed to nurses from the UK, I decided it was time to visit the mother country - England, to work and experience Britain. I was even more enthused when I learnt that I had the option of working in either Scotland or Wales too. The world certainly seemed to be my oyster and I was about to embrace it even more! So, I revived my registration process with the UKCC and successfully registered. I was soon offered a job in the UK, via a UK Nursing Recruitment Agency.

In December 1998, I arrived in the UK with my work permit, to commence a long-held dream of working in the UK as a nurse. I had a job, which came with accommodation. This was to work as the 'sister' (a senior / charge nurse) in a very posh private nursing home in the South of England. In addition to my accommodation, I was provided with meals.

All I needed to do, was to save my money to get the things I needed and boy, did I have dreams of things I needed? I did not have any outgoing expenses when I first arrived so that was very interesting – a novelty that was never before, or again experienced! However, as soon as I landed in the UK, I decided I needed to get started with continuing my education. At the time when I trained as a nurse in Jamaica, the training qualification was a Certificate and professional qualification as a Registered General Nurse (RGN).

This was the same for midwifery training. Both programmes mimicked the original UK curriculum. So, having arrived in England, I decided I would love to get a degree. I just wanted one - "how wonderful it would be to have a degree", I thought! Nowadays, the training courses in Jamaica offer degree nursing programmes routinely.

In 2009 nursing became an all-degree profession in England, meaning that all student nurses are now educated at universities in England. I discovered the Open University (OU) as soon as I got there and, hey presto! I registered with the Open University and started a course in health services management. It was very interesting to do such a course and I got to learn a bit more about the national health services in the UK – the sacred 'NHS', a national treasure, I soon learned.

One of the things that prompted me to do this course was because I had worked in supervisory/management positions whilst I was in Jamaica, including as a midwife. This was by default, a senior role at the time as one was required to first train as a general nurse. As I explained earlier, for most of us nurses, studying midwifery was an added course to

Chapter 7

promote your career whether or not you wanted to be a midwife – so I had done so. In addition, I had also worked in a supervisory position in the Cayman Islands.

So, I wanted to have a management qualification and what better area to study this than in Health Services Management, which at that time would have had the double benefit of introducing me to the nature of health services in the UK. So that was what I did. I started doing that course straight away as a part-time programme with the OU and successfully completed it. The qualification was a 'professional certificate' in health services management. I think there was the option to progress to a diploma and possibly a degree but at the time I just wanted to start something; I just wanted to have that management qualification. This was not the area in which I wanted to study for a degree.

In all honesty, I cannot say that the management qualification in Health Services did anything to progress my nursing career in the UK; however, the exposure and the motivation it provided was worth it. I have often heard it said that a major part of being successful in anything is to 'show up'. I showed up and kept showing up – meaning I stuck at a task started despite concurrently adjusting to life and working in the UK and that was a sure sign – even if I did not acknowledge it then, that I had the stamina to persevere, even in the UK. It was a new environment with all, well maybe not ALL, but still a lot of the innate challenges of moving and living somewhere new.

My formal education and professional qualifications afforded me some advantages – as explained earlier, but it was still a humongous challenge! Life progressed in England and soon I started to think that something else needed to be done. Here I was, turning 30 and my proverbial biological clock was seriously ticking! I needed to start thinking about a family and so though I was not actively looking, I realised and was very cognizant that I needed a life partner.

Shortly after my arrival in the UK, I learnt that I needed to get a 'Social Security Number'. Hence, whilst I was working in the South of England, we went to the regional office to get this National Insurance number. On our way back, my friend and I were on the train, a strange set of circumstances resulted in us meeting the young man who would become my husband.

You would never guess what. Six months after we met, we got married. I will hasten to say I did not get married because I needed to be married to stay in the country. Remember, I arrived in the UK on a work permit. I was independent. I had a work permit which allowed me to work and remain in the country legally and after working for several years I

Chapter 7

could apply for resident status and then British Citizenship. We got married simply because we were in love and wanted to be together. Many individuals find themselves forced to be married because of economic or other social reasons but, fortunately, that was not the case for me.

Looking back, one of, if not the true reason why we did get married so quickly was that we wanted to be together and as a practising Christian girl with my firm and sound Jamaican Christian country girl roots, there was no way I was about to support the commonly practised and accepted arrangement in the UK of cohabiting before marriage. I was in no way perfect but there were some principles that meant a lot to me and I was not about to abandon them – even here in the UK where at that time, I was almost invisible, coming from the Cayman Islands on my own, hardly knowing anyone.

In life, I believe, it is important that individuals have what I call 'red lines' - perhaps I've got that phrase from the Brexit era, and that was one that I was not willing to renege on. My father and my church had taught me that I must be the man's wife before I agreed to live with him, and I embrace that. So that decision was taken and on the 31st of July, the following year - 1999, six months after we met, we got married. We had a wonderful wedding day. It was a wonderful summer day, a hot, sunshine-filled day, surrounded by relatives that I hadn't seen for a long time. I found most of my relatives in England, especially aunties that I hadn't seen for a while.

As I explained previously, following mummy's death, people we were close to, including relatives, unfortunately scattered. Mummy was somehow the cohesive force in the family, so individuals went their separate ways after she died. I had not seen my aunties or indeed their offspring - my cousins. It was joyous to reunite, so that added to our wedding day being as enjoyable and as special as it was. By December 2000 we welcomed our first bouncing (yes, he was bouncing from the moment he grasped that he could) baby boy and our second by the end of November 2002. We had our two lovely, wonderful Princes. Emmanuel was a 'planned baby' because we wanted to have our first child shortly after we got married.

I was 30, my husband two years younger. Thankfully, fertility was not an issue and I became pregnant straight after we started trying. Caleb's arrival fits a bit more in the category of a 'pleasant surprise' in the sense that I was still breastfeeding Emmanuel when I became pregnant with him. I had returned to work, after a very short maternity leave, still breastfeeding Emmanuel but was also taking the contraceptive pill.

Chapter 7

That is the progesterone-only contraceptive pill which allowed me to breastfeed whilst taking the contraceptive pill. I was on night duty as a nurse and sometimes I would go to work with the pill in my pocket and return home with it in the same place, having forgotten to take it, due to being busy at work. I am unsure why I had planned to take it in the evenings; not sure what the rationale was but there must have been a good one because I am a usually a rational person.

Looking back, it is one of the best things that happened as I do not know when we would have planned to have our second child. So, we were glad he came along at the time he did; they are 23 months apart, almost two years, which is fabulous. They have grown up together and have had fun together as well as many 'bust ups'. My two not-so-little anymore Princes! They are doing well, now adults.

Church at this time was also going very well. As outlined earlier, the church is always an integral part of my life and means a significant amount to me. I am part of the church and 'church life' was my lifestyle. No matter how I appear to be prospering in the other areas of my life, if the spiritual side of my life is not developing, I cannot feel satisfied. I feel off balance; lacking good equilibrium. So overall, life for me was thriving. My husband and I were both members of the church we had started attending in Moss Side, Manchester - vibrant and teeming with life. When we first started attending, we hardly knew anyone there but we soon became a part of this wonderful church family and I was soon appointed as the Women's Ministry leader for the local church and later I became the District Women's Ministry leader.

That was something I enjoyed thoroughly; we had some lovely times. It meant that I was contributing in a very meaningful way. I recall we would have periodic women's social meetings. I think they were probably held bi-monthly. We would meet and discuss a variety of topics; it was just wonderful! The women's department was thriving; I was happy and things were going well. In addition, I was using my talents and gifts in other ways. I would be singing at church and I would sometimes deliver the Sunday morning sermon. Those things really made me feel fulfilled. The icing on the cake was that my husband was also doing very well there.

He too was thriving in church. When I first met him, he had not too long before that become a Christian in Nigeria but he also became assimilated very well into that church and was also growing very well spiritually. Shortly after we got married, my husband did a course in computer engineering and qualified as a computer systems engineer. Being from a very privileged family background, my husband's challenges growing up were a bit

Chapter 7

different from mine! After completing a private school education, he went on to university but did not complete his degree at the time for various reasons, certainly not due to academic challenges – he is very academically able! As I got to know him, I realised he had what I referred to as "huge potential". He was very smart.

I thought he had a degree because he initially led me to think so. I soon realised he did not. We agreed that he would acquire his degree later, which he did. After completing the computer course, he got a job as a computer systems engineer. Shortly after acquiring that job, he became the director for the Community Centre which is associated with the church but served the entire Moss Side community.

He was instrumental in building a computer suite and the Community Centre also served as an IT Education Centre. Various activities continued to be carried out at the Centre which was essentially a community hub.

The Centre's revenue also increased considerably because of the additional input from him. He was doing very well and I was very pleased. There was also the bonus that his salary was commensurate with the work and this meant an increase in our joint income. God's favour was on us and life was dealing us a kind hand. During this time I was studying for my degree - I was well on my way to getting my first degree! Once we were married, I had moved to Manchester where Simon was living. I secured a job as a staff nurse at the Manchester Royal Infirmary. This is a very big hospital and that was an eye-opener with a big challenge, assimilating into this new role.

However, here I was - now a nurse working in one of the big hospitals in the mother country and it was all going well. Hence, to carry on fulfilling my dream of acquiring that elusive degree, I started working night shifts. I studied part time so I would go to University, two days per week and worked about three nights per week or something similar.

But it all fitted in very well; I was getting on with my family life; my husband was doing well; church was going well; and I was on my way with my academics. I mentioned my two boys earlier; these two boys were born during the first and third years of my degree course. One colleague looked at me at one point and said, "Carol you just need to open a book to get pregnant!" To many, it seemed I was always pregnant whilst at university.

So, the boys were born whilst I was at University. As usual, I really applied myself and was rewarded. I graduated with a first-class honours degree in community health nursing. There were three or four pathways that one could follow along this degree course and I chose to follow the pathway of

Chapter 7

becoming a General Practice Nurse. The other options were to become a district nurse, a health visitor or, I think, a specialist learning disabilities nurse. Now qualified as a General Practice Nurse, my thoughts went back to my ambition to become a Nurse Practitioner.

Prior to my emigrating from Jamaica there was a very well-defined pathway to achieving this qualification there - perhaps a Masters Degree from my recollection and the role was well recognised nationally. Everyone in Jamaica knows what /who the Nurse Practitioner is. When working in that role, one undertakes certain tasks routinely and is also a prescriber. e.g., managing minor illnesses without the need for a doctor's input. Unfortunately, when I arrived in England, that role wasn't as well defined as it was in Jamaica and the General Practice Nurse pathway was as close as I could have got to it at the time when I did my first degree.

There were similarities in the role, for example managing chronic diseases and working in the general practice or community setting but I was not a prescriber, so the role lacked the autonomy that the Nurse Practitioner in Jamaica clearly had. Becoming a prescriber would require me doing another course. Nevertheless, I enjoyed this role as a General Practice Nurse. I particularly liked the setting, more so than working in a hospital. Knowing me, I had started planning the next step and that was, "Well, okay I am going to complete the prescribing course and I'll just work my way up and do whatever I need to do to be able to be recognised as a Nurse Practitioner here in England." So, I continued to work my way towards my goal with my plan in my mind on how to progress.

Once I qualified as a General Practice Nurse, I acquired a highly desirable role with the local Primary Care Trust (PCT). The Practice Nurses in this role were responsible for ensuring that all the primary care services in the area were being delivered to a very high standard.

That meant carrying out and managing the nursing care in some GP surgeries. In the area of the city where I was working there were some GP surgeries that were 'struggling' for various reasons, primarily due to staffing issues. These practices did not have a regular Practice Nurse which threw up a number of challenges for both the GPs and their staff, as well as for the patients. Where necessary, we were expected to devise policies and protocols and work with the GP and Practice Manager to generally enhance the service the practice was offering.

The grade of nursing that I was working at then, was a 'G' grade. As a staff nurse, I had started out in the hospital as a 'D' grade nurse - the first level of a qualified nurse. So, I had moved up quite a few

Chapter 7

levels. That was quite a jump for me in about three years.

Having come to the UK with great expectations, I was moving up the career ladder and everything else was in place. This was indeed a time that I felt things were going right. I was in the land of success; here in the mother country, I had proven myself as a staff nurse and had even managed to get promoted from a D grade to an E grade before I left secondary care in hospital to become a General Practice Nurse in Primary Care.

It was an interesting journey before I left secondary care trying to get promoted from a D grade to an E grade nurse on the ward. I was performing the role of an E grade, that is, as a senior staff nurse for a few months before I got appointed. Initially I was told that there were not any vacancies, even though on every night shift that I went to work I was in charge of the ward that I was on, essentially working as the E grade nurse. I decided I would leave that particular ward as there was officially no 'E grade nurse' vacancy and applied for an E grade post on another ward where a vacancy was advertised.

I turned up at the interview and my deputy ward manager was present on the panel of interviewers. I do not know whether that was planned or it was done hastily on the realisation by my ward manager and deputy manager that I was applying for another role which meant I would have resigned from my ward. However, I was offered the post of E grade Staff Nurse and it was on my existing ward doing the job that I was doing every night! It was indeed a rather bizarre but delightful turn of events.

There is a common saying amongst us Christians that, "God works in mysterious ways...!" I believe that if one puts in the effort; continues to be faithful in doing the things that he or she is purposed to do, then the door opens and things fall into place. So, the picture in the jigsaw puzzle began to emerge.

I had accomplished becoming a senior staff nurse on the ward whilst studying part time at university, completed my degree program and was now moving into the community to take up my G grade post. I worked as a Practice Nurse for only 18 months because soon I started having itchy feet and was about to move on and take yet another huge step in my quest to continue achieving success.

Chapter 7

"Success sometimes looks and feels different from what you imagine but it does not necessarily mean that it is not the same success you were pursuing..."

Chapter 8

Crisis... Relationship cracks!

I had this crazy idea that would not go away. Becoming a Nurse Practitioner was what I allowed myself to dream of achieving or becoming but was that truly the extent of my dream?

After the success I achieved with my first degree, I seriously contemplated studying law. I could have easily converted to a graduate entry LLB course with my First Class Honours degree. However, I later discarded the idea. Deep down I felt that being a nurse was probably not all that I truly wanted ultimately; I just felt there was something more. I had embarked on a nursing career to fulfil an unfulfilled dream of my late mother.

But having done it, would I allow myself the freedom to pursue my own true dream? Dare I even express it? This idea of something more was planted in my head on several occasions, going back to when I lived in the Cayman Islands. A friend of mine insisted on referring to me periodically as Dr... He said he could see 'something' in me; it was about my 'can do' attitude and the diligence with which I embraced my work.

Chapter 8

This was not particularly strange to me because I had planned to do a PhD degree at some point. Then one day I had a conversation with one of the doctors who was responsible for the medical care of the patients in the nursing home where I was one of the nurse supervisors. We chatted and he just casually mentioned that his younger brother aspired to become a doctor like him.

He told me about the challenges of getting into medical school and bemoaned the fact that some individuals do not actually get the opportunity to fulfil their dreams, specifically, to become a doctor in this case. Then with a kind of 'throw away' comment, he turned and looked at me and said, "You're happy with your career; you've become a nurse and you want to be a nurse," and I said, "Yeah".

It was true then but the more I replayed that conversation and that comment in my mind, the more I realised that if I was honest, I was not at the time truly fulfilled with regard to my career. I had started to become a bit uneasy myself about my career. The doctors I was working with whilst in the Cayman Islands always seemed to treat me as an 'equal' colleague. This was different from my experience working in Jamaica where there was a more definite tribal divide between nurses and doctors. It was a thing that existed and was perpetuated in the hospital setting; for me, not in a malicious way. It was just the way things were. As nurses, most times we got along extremely well with the doctors we worked with. This was especially so in our autonomous role as midwives when I worked in the Antenatal Clinic and particularly on the Labour Ward. However, you always somehow know your place as the nurse / midwife, not quite equal to 'the doctor'.

Perhaps because the ultimate responsibility for the patient lies with the doctor; we could always escalate an issue of clinical management of our patient to the doctor. The three main doctors I worked with in Cayman were different in their attitudes and really embraced my knowledge, skills and experience as a nurse. I felt safe to express my opinion regarding patient care and to make suggestions regarding their management that would be integrated in the patient's medical care. In the words of one of these doctors, who was older and not afraid to compliment a young nurse, "You are very clever".

On one occasion, when we were all planning to attend a seminar for varied clinicians, I discussed the topic to be taught with one of the doctors as I was curious. He told me about some pertinent areas on the topic that I should seek clarity about.

He jokingly said, "You will be viewed as being outstanding if you communicate in this way and ask

Chapter 8

these questions because most clinicians at your level, even some doctors, do not think like that." It was true, as nurses, we were trained to operate in a certain way – more utilising a protocol-driven framework than in an independent problem-solving way.

Simply because, as mentioned earlier, in the settings that I worked, the ultimate responsibility for the patient's care lay with the doctor and we could always escalate any concerns identified. This in no way means that as a nurse / midwife, I was not capable of critical thinking – far from it!

I read further on the subject and cannot recall how the actual seminar went but that little tutorial stayed with me. I now realise that those affirmative words and the general attitude of my medical colleagues during that time of my life profoundly affected the way I saw myself and the way I dared to dream, even if I did not actively acknowledge it or pursue any changes in my career path at that time – a seed was definitely planted!

As mentioned earlier, I became a nurse because my mother who had died when I was only 10 years old wanted to be a nurse and so I took up that mantle and ran with it. I had not thought about anything else and perhaps even if I had, my circumstances would not have allowed me to go to medical school at that time. Certainly, from a financial point of view, my father was not able to afford the fees. I became a nurse and I was very happy with that achievement. I had fulfilled what I set out to do. I realised, however, that I was doing every nursing course I could; that is every developmental course that would enhance my abilities and feed my constant yearning to learn more, become more. Essentially, I was unfulfilled, though I did not necessarily see it as such then.

That explains why I wanted to get going as soon as I got to England. I wanted to do this management course and having done that, this degree and now qualified as a Community Specialist Practitioner, I still wanted to do something! My rationale at this point was that I was still unable to prescribe which meant that I still had to go to the doctors that I was working with to ask them to prescribe medications for the patients that I consulted with in my capacity as a Practice Nurse, managing chronic diseases.

For example, I would know exactly what medicine I needed to give my patients with asthma whose symptoms were not well controlled or that patient with diabetes whose blood sugar levels were not satisfactory because the HbA1C was not optimised. However, I could not just prescribe the medication, I had to go to the doctor to request it and on several occasions, it meant that I had to stand at the door outside the doctor's room and wait for him / her to complete seeing their current patient,

Chapter 8

whilst my patient was also waiting. That often consumed my already limited time and was rather frustrating.

Hence, the seed planted in my mind began to take root somewhat. Maybe I could look to become a doctor. That was one way to solve that problem, permanently. Fortunately, my now germinating seed seemed to have found good soil and continued sprouting. I met someone at a nursing agency office where I went for an interview because I was looking to do some extra nursing shifts.

This young lady was applying to do extra nursing shifts as well. We got talking and I learnt that she was a recently qualified nurse but was currently at medical school. I became really fascinated and delved more into the conversation, asking her all the questions that I needed answers to.

She told me about this 'accelerated four-year medical programme' which admitted people who had nursing and or other allied health professional degree qualifications or other science degrees, to medical school. However, there were some very strict criteria to get onto this programme. For example, your first degree had to be a first-class or an upper second class. Thankfully, I had obtained a first -class honours degree so would qualify at the first academic hurdle. She explained the process would include getting through an interview, even after jumping through the initial academic 'hoops'. I went home, brimming with all this information. What would I do? The thought hit me that it seemed a real possibility that I could get into medical school.

My husband was equally excited but cautious about the prospect. He assured me that he would be willing to support me if I decided to go down that route. Now the ball was in my court. Was I going to take a shot – win or lose? It was scary but I was tingling with excitement! We had just bought a lovely house in Flixton – a desirable village in Old Trafford (near Manchester).

Having moved from the council estate where our circumstances forced us to live for a while shortly after getting married (that is another story!), it would be a wrenching experience to give up the stability that we had only recently come into, to commence another protracted period of uncertainty for us. I had the sobering realisation that this would not just affect me but had implications for my entire family. Making such major life changing decisions, especially with a young family, was not to be underestimated and I understood that.

Another thing that had also prompted me was the fact that my clinical supervisor and mentor during my practice nursing training also encouraged me to consider doing medicine. I really respected this nurse; she was super! She was one of the best nurses

Chapter 8

I have ever come across even to this day, particularly with regard to her clinical skills and expertise.

After I finished my practice nurse training and was coming to the end of the course, I began planning my next move. My plan was to go on to doing the master's degree programme in clinical nursing which would qualify me as a nurse practitioner. I contacted the university that was recommended as offering the most reputable of these courses and requested the curriculum.

They sent it to me and I scrutinised it. The course consisted of a significant number of clinical skills that we would not usually perform as nurses, even at the level I was then. I shared the curriculum and my thoughts with my mentor, commenting that it was as if you were studying to be a doctor by doing the course.

She looked at me and said, "So why don't you study medicine then?" I must have responded with some redundant comment but seriously thought, "If she thinks I can do it, then maybe I could". My reassurance came from the fact that she was a Caucasian nurse who was familiar with the English system and was very serious about her endorsements.

I just felt that if she had the confidence in me to study to that level then maybe I should do so. That moment had also significantly contributed to my germinating seed. Sometimes our mentors and encouragement come from unlikely sources.

As a black woman in a 'strange' country, having grown up in Jamaica, experiencing such positive endorsements was fuel for my self-image. Coupled with having high expectations about what the mother country could offer, I did not find it difficult to embrace this positivity and so I took it on board and pondered my mentor's comments.

With all these factors coupled with the promise of support from my husband, I decided to formally explore the possibility of studying medicine by doing this four-year accelerated course. I applied to a few medical schools via the national Universities and Colleges Admissions Services (UCAS) which is the process to follow in the UK and "lo and behold!", I was offered a place at Leicester Medical School at the University of Leicester.

This final offer came after doing the interviews which meant travelling to Leicester for the first time, not knowing where I was going but knowing my history, that was not such a feat. After all, I had travelled from Windsor to Kingston, Kingston to the Cayman Islands, and then to England all on my own! So, despite the element of unfamiliarity, this

Chapter 8

was no great feat. I accepted the offer and there I was, becoming a doctor - moving house; my husband and I uprooting ourselves and our young family from Old Trafford and our community in Manchester to take on something that was foreign, intimidating, unknown and (the COVID-19 descriptive pandemic word) – UNPRECEDENTED!

There was something else - a major part of the jigsaw puzzle. How would Simon fit into all of this? After all, he would now need to become the major bread winner. My husband had set up himself and had become the director of the Community Project in Manchester. He was on a decent salary and things were looking good.

We had become part of this lovely church community and everything seemed perfect. But we were in this together, it was not just my dream; we were doing this as a duo and taking our boys along with us. We had even received the blessings of our immediate families – as terrified as they seemed. But they knew we were a formidable team and would accomplish what we set out to do if we stuck together by continuing to support each other and our family.

Simon voiced the reality to me that, "This is going to be one of the most difficult things we do together," but we were not deterred. Everything else aside, we knew how to pray together. In addition to the success of personal achievement and fulfilment, becoming a doctor had other benefits. Achieving that status was something that would put our family into another echelon of society, because it meant increased earnings and social standing. Whether we like it or not, the reality of our society is that these things count. In addition, I was thinking 'in the back of my mind' that my husband at some point would be studying as well so I would get the chance to support him when his time came around.

Needless to say, it was a tough start. We moved into a rented property in Leicester because we did not want to buy until we had a better 'feel' for the area. The house itself was a challenge as it was, shall we say, a few steps down from our lovely home that we had sold and walked away from in Flixton, Old Trafford.

We had just a few days to find that property before I actually started Medical School and we were also competing with the clock to get the boys into a suitable nursery in Leicester - something that we were not willing to compromise on, so other things were a lower priority and had to be worked around the boys' nursery in relation to my university location. But we managed it, though frantically!

Simon landed a dream job at Leicester City Council. It was perfect for his skill sets that he had developed over the years but particularly during his

Chapter 8

time, developing and managing the Community Centre in Manchester. There was some element of flexibility that the job offered, allowing us to juggle childcare, particularly, between us dropping off and picking up the boys from nursery. It all just seemed to work out perfectly. Pheeww! Thank God.

So, I arrived at medical school. I thought, "Yes Carol you have done this; you're so blessed; you are highly favoured; you've got your family; got your degree; you've got years of nursing experience and yeah, you got into medical school!" Then I had an awakening – Oh, my Lord, are these people at medical school brilliant or what? They told us in no uncertain terms during our induction period that, "All of you here are in the top 1% of the brightest people in the country; you are the cream of the crop".

We were told that being a medical student was no ordinary feat and made to feel like the elite in this society. In a sense, this was true. WE had worked our hardest and had overcome what many failed to overcome; achieved what many would not have put themselves through; the discomfort of achieving what we did to get here.

There were some people who took that very literally and even to the end of our tenure at medical school behaved like the cream of the crop – not in gracious ways but in an "in your face, look at me" demeanour. The way I saw it, we were still who we were – including one girl, coming from 'Windsor country bottom' in rural Jamaica and so, needed to keep her feet on the ground.

So here is the score: "If I thought I was 'bright', goodness me, there were some bright people at medical school!" To compound the issue, these bright people did not have two children ages one and three years old and a husband to cater to whilst studying medicine. Most of these much younger people had recently completed their first degrees, maybe worked for a couple of years in their jobs and had always wanted and been working towards getting into medical school. They were driven, motivated and mostly from more stable financial circumstances than I was.

Some had wealthy parents from wealthy backgrounds because, let's face it, typically medical school places go to people from this stratum of society. It was less pronounced in my immediate group of graduate entrants on the Accelerated Four-Year Medical Course, but this reality was ubiquitous in this setting as the traditional five-year programme medical students were also around.

I realised I was in a different world, in a different league, in a different realm. This fact was to become even more apparent as I moved up the ranks in my medical career. Medical school was tough - the

Chapter 8

workload was voluminous, it was humongous! Yet I was determined and I was ploughing my way through, come what may. I would be up nights; whilst studying the washing machine would be going. I tried to fit in everything that I could whilst reading, completing assignments and course work or preparing for an exam until around 04:00.

Then I would sleep until about 06:00, get up and help my husband to get the boys ready for nursery. He usually dropped them off whilst I would have maybe another hour or so to eat and get myself ready before I would walk to medical school which was nearby. Hence, a major reason why we had chosen the house we had rented. I was not driving at the time. Since arriving in the UK, getting a UK driving licence was one thing that kept eluding me! But have you noticed that I did not allow that so-called barrier to prevent me from moving on?

So, I would be the one to pick up the boys from nursery at the end of my medical school day whilst most of my colleagues would head home to revise or maybe go for a cheeky 'chill out' session in the pub or somewhere relaxing.

My life revolved around Medical School, home, family life and church on the weekend. For the most part I was happy with that. It was the price I had to pay and I was willing to pay it. My husband started getting uneasy and began to complain that I was not showing him enough attention or giving him enough time. Our relationship started showing cracks big time. Things just got bad and I began to question myself about my decision. He asked me whether I would take some time out of medical school. This was heartbreaking for me, but I was desperate to save my marriage and to keep my family intact.

I made an appointment with one of the pastoral Deans of the Medical School. I remember her name - Mrs Oppenheimer. She was a consultant obstetric surgeon who worked part time in that capacity at the Medical School at that time.

I went into Mrs. Oppenheimer's office and I told her I was contemplating taking a year out of medical school. She looked at me and said, "Carol, what I can tell you is that most people who take time out never come back." The rest of the conversation was around the premise that it was ultimately my decision as to what I did but with encouragement to fight to carry on and finish the course if I could.

After our meeting, I thought long and hard: those poignant words kept ringing in my ears and I mulled them over and over – "Most people who leave never come back". Let us face it, what would I realistically do during the year of time out? I would have had to find a job as I still needed to contribute to our finances. Whilst at Medical School, I was on a

Chapter 8

bursary and occasionally did some shifts with the nursing agency that I was signed up with, but these were limited, for obvious reasons. Nevertheless, I had continued to contribute to our family finances, though my husband was now the main breadwinner. I was also forced to get a professional study loan from the bank to help cover our living costs, primarily the cost of the children's nursery fees as these were, as usual totally exorbitant!

Essentially, giving up medical school would not mean a period where I could relax at home and be the perfect wife and mother as financially we were only just getting by... or could I have reorganised the whole thing and made it work? What would my mental state of mind be during the period?

How would I perceive my husband? Would I have resented him? What if I did really end up not returning to medical school? What if? What if? I remember when I was about to leave Manchester for medical school, so many people were 'rooting' for me. Many women were depending on me to blaze this path.

I recall one person in particular - Carla - who said to me, "Carol, you are a pioneer: whatever you do, please remember you're doing this for many women." She reminded me of my journey and that this was a path rarely trodden by the likes of me or us - a black woman from Jamaica who came to the

UK to work as a nurse. I had felt proud and confident and scared all at the same time. I knew there was a big possibility that I could 'fail', at least that is how it would be perceived by many if I did not complete the course and graduate as a doctor.

I was taking on this tremendous task and when she spoke those words to me, I had thought, "Oh my God, I can't let down all these people, I can't let down myself." Now, as I prayed desperately and reminisced about those words and that conversation, I thought, I came here to do this. I need to finish it. "It's the finishing!" So, I thought, "You know what, I'm gonna carry on, I'm gonna finish this." So, I made the decision to carry on and complete my course.

It was a decision that had an impact upon my marriage, but I knew, either way, it would have been affected and we had to work through it. I decided I was not willing to give up this dream and this opportunity that had been given to me, simply because times got tough. I was getting through the hours of studying and passing the exams. On some occasions I had to resit exams, but I was getting through. The support was there from the medical school and I needed to embrace it.

Therein lies a difference between the support system in my home country and the system here in England - at least, as I had known it in Jamaica. One

Chapter 8

admirable thing about being in medical school in England was that I had access to a lot of support resources, in various forms, whether it were finances or psychological support. I did not need more than these in the capacities that I mentioned earlier but it meant that these things were available when I needed them. Even if I had to pay back the loan, it was not a problem, for me the bottom line was that I was able to access these facilities when I needed them. Repaying was for the future, a bridge I would cross when I got here.

The ensuing journey was anything but easy. We faced challenges not suitable for analyses within the context of this story, but we decided to carry on. My husband continued to support me and we worked through a very difficult period. I graduated as a qualified doctor in July 2008 after starting the course in 2004. I had managed to complete the course in the recommended four years; I did not have to re-sit another year.

This time I did not graduate with first class honours but that was not important to me; I graduated, having successfully completed my medical degree. I even managed to get some merits in two of my final exams – a written and practical exam each. My goodness, wasn't this amazing? Wasn't this fantastic? It was hallelujahs and praises and fist bumps and hoorays, and everybody was rejoicing with me and my family - no one more so than my husband. We had done it; we had worked hard; we had done it and now my children's mother had become a doctor; my husband's wife was now a doctor. I would say to myself, Carol, you are now a doctor!

My father and siblings were equally as proud and emotional as could be. It was sad my mother was not here to celebrate with us, at least, not physically! We all acknowledged it was a fantastic achievement: we were still together as a family unit, and I was still in church, though I had to step back for a while, but I was still a part of this very meaningful family unit. I was truly grateful. My goodness: who says a woman cannot have it all?

I paused here to reminisce and contextualise - here I was, coming from my beloved rural and particularly remote Windsor District in Jamaica, without any modern amenities or even proper roads. Against all odds, I had made it to England and become a doctor. Wow!

Moreover, I had not abandoned a fundamental and key pillar of my life - I was still a God-believing, God- trusting Christian. For many, that little detail may not mean much but it was a big deal for me! Now, what would be next? I would definitely allow myself to bask in this achievement for a while but not to rest on my laurels – in fact, I could not, even if I wanted to.

Chapter 8

Now it was time to go out into the world and prove that I did not just have the qualifications of a doctor, but that I could work as a doctor and show myself to be a very good doctor, indeed! I was determined to be the best. This is when I draw on my life's motto again: "I can do all things through Christ who strengthens me." (Philippians 4:13)

"Sometimes opposition comes from the unlikeliest of places, but we must always be gracious and not be quick to judge. Your journey does not only affect you but potentially everyone around, especially those you are close to."

Chapter 9

The Onset of the 'Junior Doctor' Years

I had pledged to be the best doctor and yes, I was determined to be.

So, I started my first job as a junior doctor. A night shift was to herald my very first shift, but listen, the day was not left for me to sleep and rest in preparation to starting my new job. The daytime consisted of a full day of induction. Could they be mad? I was meant to do a full day of induction, learning all the practicalities of working as a new doctor in the NHS, then go home, get changed and go back to work, to work the night as a junior doctor - my very first night; my very first shift!

Missing the induction session was not an option. It is true that we had worked on the wards as medical students during our training but working independently as a junior doctor would be a different ball game in many ways and one hoped that one would at least be given the chance to prepare in the best way possible. There were many practical things that required arranging, such as my 0computer login details for the various electronic platforms that we use in hospitals. I had no idea about some of the routines of the job during the night-time. Much information was given during the induction, but they were just theory. I had no idea who I'd be working with; it was a good recipe for anxiety and panic, but I mustered everything in me to remain calm and deal with this mini-crisis strategically.

We had been warned on many occasions that we would be thrown in at the deep end - and my word, wasn't this the epitome of being thrown in at the deep end? A baptism of fire, certainly. Nevertheless, I went home, probably had an hour's sleep and went back with fear and trepidation to begin my first shift as a junior doctor on that night in August 2008.

I was working with a surgical registrar (Dr M) as a Foundation Year 1 (FY1) surgical team doctor. That first night turned out to be not as bad as I had thought it would be - pheeww! The key factor was that I had a good, compassionate and supportive registrar to work with and supervise me. In the UK a registrar (Specialist Registrar) is a doctor who is next in line to the consultant.

These doctors would have completed several years in their training journey following graduation from medical school. Following graduation, they would have completed two years of foundation training in general medicine and surgery (such as I was embarking on) and then commence their area of specialist training. In Dr M's case, maybe he had done about six years post-graduation, at the level he

Chapter 9

was at. He was kind and understanding. I was to learn that he was somewhat of a rare breed at his stage, in this speciality. Dr M took into consideration that it was my first night and first shift as a junior doctor.

So, we got through the night and I survived. The pattern continued and for the most part, I enjoyed my first 2 weeks as a junior doctor, doing the night shift surgical rotation. However, being on night shift meant that I missed the first two weeks of day duty with my teammates in the group that I was assigned to for the first rotation which was a four-month period.

During this time, my colleagues were learning the ropes, that is, the routines and idiosyncrasies of this particular surgical team. It is worth bearing in mind that all routine surgical procedures took place during the day; the bulk of my duties on the night shifts would be managing surgical admissions and urgent and emergency cases. Though extremely valuable experience, it was different from the routines of working during the daytime.

Unfortunately, when I got back to the team two weeks later, I felt I was on many occasions treated as if it were my fault that I had not been around during the first two weeks to learn the routines and I had to overcome another mountain in coming to terms with these. It was a case of "Oh you don't know how to do this, you don't know that this works that way, you don't know that we meet at this time at this place, you don't know where such and such a room is that we go to after the ward round in the morning to allocate the jobs and have a cup of tea and some toast if we are lucky!"

To put it bluntly, there was not much sympathy shown and I realise this was a different world, maybe because it was the world of the surgeons? Or simply the world of doctors? I quickly learnt that doctors are a different breed, perhaps because of the untold amount of stress that we must learn to cope with. It is crucial to be as resilient as possible and this means no 'spoon feeding'.

I think this is where the real baptism of fire started; it was far worse than the night shifts at the beginning. There was one female registrar who was the hardest taskmaster of them all! Why? one asks oneself. Is this about a woman demonstrating that she belongs and can be as good or as harsh as any man can be? I certainly was not impressed but in this arena my opinion did not matter a lot.

Let us rewind. I entered medical school as an experienced and accomplished grown woman at age 35. When I started my first junior doctor's role, I was almost 40 years old and had a previous career which span 13 years of being a nurse and midwife and included years of working as a senior nurse.

Chapter 9

That reality seemed to disappear overnight. I was now the junior doctor in the presence of my seniors - the almighty consultant surgeons AND Miss X. She was one of the registrars in the team, but she was the only woman at that level and was not to be overlooked!

In my eyes, her demeanour was rather cold and calculating – as one who was out to get to the top and would not care if she crushed you in the process. It was just a very volatile and uncertain environment – one of the worst that I have ever worked in, as a nurse or as a doctor. For me, it was toxic. It is well documented that the environment for junior doctors in the NHS can be quite a gruelling and harsh one.

Unfortunately, individuals have even resorted to taking their own lives due to the pressures. It was a sort of pressure that is beyond explanation; one must experience it to understand it. On the one hand, you are in this very privileged place, but you are often made to feel like a nobody. Coupled with the pressure and expectation to deliver, it can become overwhelming, especially for people who are accustome always to be delivering to very high standards and feel they may have failed at doing so for one reason or another, which is inevitable in medicine. I remember one day I stood in front of the consultants, registrars and my other junior doctor colleagues to hand over a patient. I felt as if my throat was closing, I felt I couldn't speak. I could not understand what was happening to me – to confident me!

It is worth bearing in mind my unique set of circumstances - remember who I am - a black woman who did not grow up in this country, an older woman aged 40 in comparison to the more common younger ages of around 23 or 24, when most junior doctors in England start their careers. I might not have looked my age, thank God, but that was my reality!

It was a culture shock; it was a change in every aspect of the word and for me required massive acclimatisation. However, I pushed on and carried on because I was determined to be the best doctor that I could be. I knew I was capable and had what it takes. I worked extremely hard and cared for my patients well; the nurses on the wards respected me for that.

Nurses are often a good 'thermometer' to gage where a junior doctor is at; they will tell you (or gossip about you) if you are not fit for purpose. Though many of the nurses were not aware, I knew that because I used to be one of them. On some occasions, they would make me a cup of tea and invite me into their exclusive 'Nurses' Room' to take a little break. On one of my weekend shifts when I was the only junior doctor on duty, the consultant

Chapter 9

covering made lovely remarks and reported to the team on my excellent performance the following Monday. Miss X's comment was only that she could not understand how you can be so brilliant on the weekend but during the week you don't seem so confident. I really wanted to tell her the answer but thought better of it.

The raging question was bursting to escape my lips: "Could it have anything to do with your presence and the way you treat people?" Or maybe certain people? Maybe, just maybe. Women are often accused of being each other's worst enemies and the first to pull each other down. I am cognisant of that reality as I write and even now I am engaged in deep introspection, just in case I am being unfair to my female senior colleague.

However, there are some truths that must be told, even if only for the sake of discussion and analysis. I recall clearly going home one day, standing, and looking into the mirror and telling myself that I was a doctor – "You are Dr Carol S. Douglas-Ighofose," I said to myself. I had begun to doubt that I was worthy of being called a doctor, in the process of proving that I was one. I had recently heard a speech where the speaker stated that success is "scarier than failure". Many do not cope well with success because there is a skill involved in managing success. Failure is often what is experienced and expected, but when success comes, many find they are unable to deal with it. That explains why so many lottery winners blow their fortunes in record time and return to their pre-winning state of being, or even, to a worse state.

Under no circumstance would squandering my success become my reality. I had worked hard to achieve it and I was going to embrace it. Moreover, I was (am) a child of God with the lifelong mantra of "I can do all things through Christ who strengthens me" (Philippians 4:13 KJV). Should I have spoken up? Maybe I should have but I do not regret not having done so. I did not think it was the right time. I believe that part of being successful is having the wisdom to act at precisely the right time despite being justified to do so at other times.

I once heard a quote from Bishop T.D. Jakes in which he stated that "Just because you have a stone, you do not have to throw it." Moreover, it is always wise to pick your fights and choose your battles. I do not think I would have won that battle and the repercussions might have been too costly at that time for me personally and for my career. I did choose to have a private 'battle' with Miss X at the end of that rotation; however, despite numerous attempts and invitations to a meeting with me, she did not rise to the challenge but simply ignored my requests. Arrogance or cowardice? Perhaps I should leave you to be the judge of that one.

Chapter 9

Nonetheless, the junior doctor's life carried on. We got to the ward every morning one or two to three hours before the ward round. The ward rounds were meant to start at about 8am or 9am but we would be there from 6am preparing and making sure every 't' was crossed and every 'i' was dotted. We would ensure that we were familiar with every patient admitted under the care of our team's consultants including any patient who was admitted overnight.

The results of investigations were checked, the patient's history was known and we endeavoured to learn everything about the patient that was worth knowing or deemed relevant so we could present our patient to the consultant in as flawless a way as possible when we stood in front of the 'demigods' on the ward rounds!

They were very petrifying experiences but the end point was that we were doing all we could to ensure that each patient got absolutely the best care and management that they could possibly receive whilst under our care. It was an admirable outcome. Even if this meant massaging the ego of someone, if our patients benefited, we would do it. I clearly recall Miss X saying to me that each patient is "my patient" – meaning that whilst that patient is under her care, she takes full ownership and responsibility for such a patient. Whilst that is admirable, there is a tone of control and arrogance that infiltrates that statement that does not quite sit very comfortably. It is subtle… "my patient" …debatable maybe.

On almost every working day we started early and we left late. That is the equivalent of many hours of unpaid work that we gave to the NHS. By now I had more than paid back the bursary I received during my training. It is true that there is no such thing as a free lunch. I am forever grateful for the opportunity I was given but make no mistake the proverbial 'pound of flesh' was taken back by our good NHS.

Not just flesh but I dare say the NHS did take back its pound of flesh with the blood supply! But we were proud and felt privileged to serve in this way. So, I continued like many before me and very likely many will follow this pattern of serving in the NHS. I went on to enjoy some super rotations in my junior doctor years. Two of my personal favourites were rotations in Psychiatry and Obstetrics and Gynaecology. I chose to mention these as I think the placement experience in both those rotations were excellent.

My psychiatry rotation was my second rotation, following the 'baptism of fire' of my first rotation. It was such a contrast. Junior doctors were treated in so much more of a humane way, that the contrast was palpable. I think God allowed the rotations to work that way as I needed that reprieve to rebuild

Chapter 9

my self-esteem and perception and restore the faith and respect I held for my senior colleagues. Arguably, psychiatry was different from surgery in the sense that it may be considered less fast- paced in its day-to-day running, unless of course there was a crisis.

However, I do think a lot has to do with the culture that has been built up around these specialities. Psychiatry can be equally demanding, particularly emotionally and mentally draining, yet the experience was so different. In my experience it was my former, rather than this emotionally charged environment that lent itself more to the risk of burnout for the junior doctor.

The junior doctors' rota coordinator in one of these rotations was excellent. I had begun to lose hope in junior doctors' rota coordinators because of the harrowing experiences that too many junior doctors are familiar with. There are documented stories of junior doctors even struggling to get time off to attend their own weddings!

In my own experience, just trying to get time off to attend my father-in-law's burial was one I would not wish to repeat. It was as if I was responsible for the man's death; it was treated as an avoidable pleasure holiday that I dared to request time off for. I ran into countless brick walls just trying to get the time off and had to organise swaps amongst my colleagues to get the time off. The recurring words from the rota co-ordinators and senior colleagues were always that it was down to me to arrange this.

You can guess how stressful such a situation can turn out to be when juggling a bereavement with an already stressful job and trying not to let the family down. This, of course, includes a partner who has lost a parent and you wanting to play your role of supporting your spouse at such a horrible time. For partners and relatives of doctors in this position, it must seem imperceivable that doctors could apparently be so heartless to each other.

These circumstances risk igniting conflict between couples when the other partner may feel they are being slighted by their partner who is not keen to support them and the family with a perceived excuse of not being able to get time off work.

Hence, such circumstances may be interpreted as the doctor elevating the job above their family's needs. In the end, one of my (junior doctor) colleagues helped me by even doing some shifts for me without me returning the favour as we just could not figure out a way to swap our times. It was that bad. I am eternally grateful to him. Those are some of the reasons why I have so much respect for the majority of my colleagues, knowing that almost every doctor does this job as a vocation. They are

Chapter 9

extremely hard-working and excellent individuals who deserve the utmost respect.

Now, there is another battle that I had to fight during this eventful period of my life. It was undoubtedly another massive element that was a generator of anxiety for me. I kept failing my driving tests! To make it worse, my husband announced that I was deliberately failing them so that I could be exempted from certain family responsibilities. Perhaps you can understand his rationale, but I struggled to. Why would I do that? Why would anyone? Absolutely absurd!

I arrived in England from the Cayman Islands where I was living and drove an automatic car. I had to retake my driving test when I needed to retain my driving licence. But somehow, I just could not pass my driving test. I even initially thought I would revert to having a licence for automatic vehicles only, but it just did not make sense and did not work out. Oh no!

I will not tell you how many attempts I had before finally passing but there were a few. Shall we say, this will be one of the mysteries of this book? Yes, I think so.

"Success is often more difficult to manage than failure.

Just because you have a stone, even if it is legitimate to do so, you do not have to throw it."

Chapter 10

Is this my Space?

I felt the need to start working part time as I wrestled with the feeling that my children were being shortchanged. I struggled with feeling that I had not spent enough time with them, had not been a part of all their school activities and you name it... I wanted to spend more time with them, so I opted to work part time in the second year of my Foundation Year (FY2) as a junior doctor, following graduation.

Unfortunately, this turned out to be only partially true as in reality our circumstances were such that I could not financially afford to genuinely work part time. In the end I spent my days off during the week looking after the children and the weekends doing locum shifts to make up our shortfall. I look back now and marvel and contemplate whether that was the best way to address our financial needs. My husband was always in charge of our finances as I felt I had too much on, working on the wards and coping with everything else at home to also manage home finances.

I relinquished those responsibilities, choosing to believe that he would do a better job than I would. Is this a mistake that women often make? The evidence seems to hold up that a lot of women tend to hand over the financial reins to their partners, despite the real-life circumstances which clearly demonstrate that women may be better at budgeting. This perhaps, holds true for women in countries where the economy is less stable and families are on a more stringent budget than in the UK or other western countries. However, I'm not sure that the evidence stacks up.

It was not without difficulties getting the approval to work part time as I was still technically on the junior doctors' training programme. It is not until one has completed his or her formal training programme as a doctor in the UK that you can truly decide independently about your work pattern and choose your work hours. The argument was that I could not be allowed to work part time as well as do locum shifts. The question I was asked is: "How can you find the time to do locum shifts if you can't work full time?"

To me the answer was simply because I did the extra shifts at the weekend when my husband had his days off, so he could look after the children. It appears the simple, commonsense answer but just did not seem to feature with those on the committee that I had to apply to, to get this arrangement approved. Perhaps it was their way of protecting me because this was no way to live on an ongoing basis. In the end, my request to work part time and to be

Chapter 10

allowed to work extra shifts at the weekend was not approved so I returned to working full time to fulfil our financial commitments. That saga made me realise even more the unique profession that medicine was… still is!

Theoretically, it rightly aims to protect you and ensure that as an individual doctor you are always in the best physical, mental and emotional state to perform maximally. However, the rota that we were given sometimes and the extra hours that we were forced to put in on a voluntary basis do not remotely account for that reality of holistic well-being. At the risk of sounding cynical, it is almost as if the welfare rules apply when it suits those in charge. However, circumstances like those made me conclude that this medical career was not supposed to be for common folks like me. I mentioned earlier that this noble profession was meant for those who were in the upper echelons of society.

This represents people who do not have financial concerns historically, who could work part time if they needed to and did not need to worry about day-to-day financial difficulties that warrant doing things like working additional hours. Their women who needed to work part time to look after their children had the financial backing of either a partner or their families and did not traditionally have to make ridiculous requests like the one I had made.

I felt I was being given a message that this space was preferably not occupied by people like me who came from abroad. It was as if you would not be allowed to come here and sit among the leaders. If you cannot do what they do you do not get to sit here. We will allow you to enter but if you cannot walk the walk and act the act then we will not allow you to remain or go further.

However, I was determined to sit firmly at this table and find a way to 'fit in' and make things work to suit my social and financial circumstances. My husband intervened again at this time with another 'brilliant' idea, shall we say. He said, now you are qualified as a doctor, stop pursuing the idea of becoming a specialist. Just give up the medical training pathway so you can have total autonomy and independence about your working hours. Essentially, just work the day job as a doctor and do not worry about training to be any specialist or about becoming a general practitioner (GP).

The truth is that after completing my FY2 programme, I could opt to do only contracted / locum shifts and just remain as a junior doctor without any formal specialist training for the rest of my medical career. I could, arguably, carve out a medical career for myself this way by doing courses that appealed to me if and when I chose, rejecting the formal training pathway. Whilst this is radical and perhaps, entrepreneurial, it is not looked upon

Chapter 10

with much admiration in our profession. It would mean foregoing the opportunity to gain any formal specialist / GP credentials and would, invariably lose the recognition amongst my medical colleagues and in my profession. In medicine, some choose such a path for various reasons and work in positions known as 'staff grade'.

This may include very well-qualified doctors from abroad who struggle to get on to the UK training programme to formalise their training which they did abroad or, simply, to retrain in the UK. The reality is that, sometimes, doctors find themselves in these precarious positions because they have come to the UK from abroad and have not had the opportunity to train in a specialty or maybe some doctors have simply taken that decision not to. However, if I decided to embrace such a pathway, the reality would be that of a more difficult life without much prospect of changing or improving.

It would mean going from hospital to hospital to work, wherever the shifts are available, and though you might get good rates of pay at some point it would be capped as you would never really be able to charge a 'specialist' rate. For me the psychological impact of not completing my medical training would have been great, especially if I felt that I was forced to 'sabotage' my medical career. If one makes that decision and perhaps decides to explore something else outside of medicine or choose an unconventional path in medicine, then that is absolutely fine, but I would not have been able to own such a decision, so it would be a problem. Yes, you guessed right: I emphatically rejected that suggestion which meant another crisis point in my relationship and, by extension, my life.

My husband proposed that our boys would be better off going to private school or face the potential of a possibly unfulfilled education career in the UK. I agreed because we were already encountering problems with the traditional educational system as it related to our two young boys. There were reports of our child beginning 'to play up' in school... you know like ethnic children do, especially boys from the African Caribbean background!

I dare say, fitting right into that slot and even at their young age at primary school, there were talks of possible exclusion because a child was "too lively", and the school was having difficulty controlling them. In the end, the diagnosis of Attention Deficit Hyperactivity Disorder came in for discussion. After much discussion, a decision was made to send both children to private schools. Was that the right decision? Even as a doctor I had issues surrounding a medical diagnosis in this situation. This is not to say that I am denying that some children have genuine medical problems which warrant formal diagnoses, but I am keen that these

Chapter 10

diagnoses are not made on a whim, especially as it pertains to ethnic minority children who may behave a little differently. It was an expensive decision to send both children to private schools, but I believe one that paid off eventually. Time will tell. My children concur to some extent, but they have interesting views – and rightly so. After all, they have been educated to be critical thinkers!

So, I finally passed my driving test! I was just so nervous during the driving tests though I could not possibly understand why those immense fears existed. There were suggestions that I consider taking medications, for example, beta blockers, just to help to suppress the adrenaline rush and help calm me down but I did not feel comfortable going down that route, though that would have been a legitimate reason for medication. Finally, I got a driving instructor whom I was very comfortable with and a driving assessor who just worked with and for me on the day of my test… and it worked! I passed my driving test.

The driving assessor on the day had no idea of my previous experiences and the prayers interceding that were offered and invested into this bizarre phenomenon of my life are not to be underestimated. It was as if I had hit upon an impossible barrier for something that seems so mundane and routine for others. Thank God it was finally torn down and overcome. However, something that happened later was quite revealing and provided me with a bit of solace. I was having difficulties in some other areas of my academic work and the decision was made that I should have further formal testing to identify any disabilities that I might not have been aware of. I knew I was not dyslexic, as we were routinely tested for those on entering medical school. Following an extensive psychological testing, it was uncovered that I possess a visual-spatial disability (which I mentioned previously).

This means that my hand-eye and general coordination is not optimum. I have always known that, but I did not think it would affect me in other ways: e.g., if you playfully throw an object at me, you'll be very lucky if I catch it. I am very awkward with things like ball games.

When I did the test, I was asked specifically how I fared with driving test situations. I was told then and there that a visual-spatial disability such as I have would have definitely affected me in the way it had. Now that I have mastered the driving it does not affect my day-to-day driving, (except I can get lost quite easily!) but mastering my driving and getting through the test would have been an issue. As it relates to my academic achievements, there are some areas of academics that this disability definitely affects, e.g., I'm not good with some forms of activities, such as matching shapes and spaces. I

Chapter 10

just do not do very well with those. Apparently, what I have done over the years is to compensate for this by developing other areas of skill. For example, I performed above average in other areas of the test, including demonstration of very highly-developed language skills.

I was advised that this would have enabled me to compensate for a lack in other areas and that's why I've been able to do so well academically even though I've got this disability. Thank God for that; there is always a way! So again, the good Lord looked after me. I am aware that I have mentioned this seemingly innocuous 'disability' repeatedly.

I have done so to draw attention to an issue that may serve as an immediate deterrent to achieving goals for many individuals. It is true that disabilities are factors that are likely to bring about crisis situations in life, and visual-spatial disabilities, though apparently harmless, affect 'everyday life' as much as academic settings. However, life has also shown us that there is always a way to overcome these crises. Whether a disability is considered minor or major, it is not a bad thing; rather, a reality of life.

Being aware of it, acknowledging it and strategising for it is another useful weapon in our armory for success. This further delineates the fact that we were made in such a wonderful way -

"fearfully and wonderfully made" as King David exuberantly declares in Psalm 139: 14. Many who are acquainted with me may appreciate the credence I give to this. It forms part of the topic of my first book! We have the God-given ability to adapt and compensate when we need to, in order to progress.

So, if we are truly determined and adapt a mindset to overcoming impediments, though there might be obstacles, we will get over them. This realisation was absolute testament to that belief. So, although it was emotional to some extent, e.g., dealing with feelings of inadequacy and crass comments such as the assertion that I was deliberately failing the driving tests to avoid some of my duties as a woman, it was a little occasion of celebration for me.

Now having the time to recollect and analyse these experiences, I have reconceptualized them as examples of crises in my life that I have managed successfully. There are some that specifically relate to my role as a woman in society, including as a wife and, or as a mother. I have not allowed those encumbrances to set me back, but rather have used them as stepping-stones to achieve my next level of development. I think I can safely say that they now exist as scars, rather than scabs.

Embarking on and executing my GP training constituted lots of battles including the need to

Chapter 10

resort to part-time training in the end, due to the insurmountable difficulties I experienced 'juggling' everything. Getting through the final exams was a novel example of failure that I experienced for the first time as well. The practical exam is very culturally based. One is advantaged by having a good understanding of the nuances of British culture.

Although I was doing well in my day-to-day practice, it was still an issue in the exam situation. This is an issue that gained the attention of the British media and was a source of investigation by the Royal College of General Practitioners (RCGP) as requested by several other professional groups. The problem was affecting a disproportionate number of doctors from ethnic minority backgrounds, especially those who came from abroad.

Again, I overcame that crisis assisted by very supportive people. One who is worth mentioning is Dr C. Duncan, my GP trainer and clinical supervisor for most of the duration of my training. She supported me through all the difficulties I faced. Dr Duncan's commitment and belief in me gave me a renewed faith in humanity and in my profession. A stalwart doctor with years of experience as a Caucasian GP in an inner-city practice, she was wise and very pragmatic. She is endowed with years of experience and clinical skills and expertise to match. I later had further support from other GP trainers who I am also eternally grateful to, but Dr Duncan will always be my heroine and I salute her quietly and pray for her on many days of my life! I do think it is important to acknowledge one's network of support and the role of one's faith in difficult circumstances. In Jamaica, growing up, we used to sing a song – "No man is an island; no man stands alone..." I used to just equate the song with Jamaica being an island... but the song is universally sung and has a significant message about the impact of humans on each other in our quest for success.

It is almost impossible for anyone to achieve success solo. We are all dependent on each other. The sooner we realise and embrace this concept, the better off we will be. This goes to the heart of our being as, in helping each other, we feel better in ourselves and achieve more by helping each other.

For me, it is the concept of service. I subscribe to the fact that we are, at our core, service beings. Along my path, I have come to know so many amazing colleagues and so many individuals have been willing to assist me in many ways, when I have, usually reluctantly, asked for help. I too am still learning that lesson and fighting to overcome that hesitancy to seek help when necessary and foster interdependence. It is good to have a certain internal locus of control but being aware and being willing to relent when it is necessary is an

Chapter 10

achievement and, for me, is a measure of confidence, which denotes an element of being truly successful.

With these elements of support as well as support from the GP training school I completed my course and qualified as a GP in 2015. Yeah! I got this! It seems, after all, I can have it all... but can I?

CAN WOMEN HAVE IT ALL?

"It is often difficult to adjust, accept and become acceptable in an elevated space. Many things will conspire to make the reality of 'imposter syndrome' a demon to battle."

Chapter 11

Success is Reflection and Gratitude

Recognising or acknowledging help and being grateful is essential. England has been good to me. Maybe, one would say, Carol has made good of what England has offered her. Whichever way it is phrased, there is much to be thankful for. But let's be clear: my ultimate source is God!

I came here uncertain of what might happen but, nevertheless, having great expectations. Of course, I would: I was coming to the motherland. The motherland is supposed to provide its children with tender care, nurturing and opportunities and I expected no less from England. There were harsh times; there were confusing times. There were difficulties assimilating into a novel country with its peculiarities and idiosyncrasies.

When my first patient in southern England said to me, "Nurse, I need to spend a penny", it took me aback momentarily, but I quickly realised what she was on about and promptly helped her to the toilet.

Similarly, as a staff nurse on the ward in Manchester, when my colleague offered me a 'butty', I was perplexed. I had no idea that she was referring to a sandwich. The 'bacon butty' I could then understand but for the life of me I could not get my head around a 'chip butty'. "You mean you put potato chips between two slices of bread and eat and enjoy that?" I asked. Well, I was fascinated... That was certainly a new concept of a sandwich – carbohydrate upon carbohydrate! She continued to bemuse me by complaining how "it was chock-a-block" on her way to work as she bemoaned the daily traffic jam.

Though I was, at times baffled, I enjoyed the 'banter' and more so the apparent mysteries in this culture, especially in the language - coming to terms with the fact that the English language of the British people did not always sound like the orations I heard on the BBC news, back in the Caribbean. The English language of the people had an array of dialects and colloquialisms probably even more so than we do in Jamaica where the patois spoken is slightly different in each parish that one resides in or that one visits. Who would have thought?

Looking back on all my achievements since emigrating here, I am grateful. Reflecting on achieving my degrees may seem routine for a lot of British people, but for me that was a significant achievement. To have ended up with more than the first-degree qualification that I was yearning for is even more reason to be grateful, considering I started out just desperate to have a degree. I was considered one of the brightest amongst my peers

Chapter 11

when I was growing up - as bright as any young person growing up in England - but I did not end up with a degree initially, simply because of the educational structure and my chosen academic pathway at the time when I studied in Jamaica. Having said that, I think it was because of the time during which I did my initial nursing qualifications as the Jamaican nursing education system was a replica of that of the British.

I believe that the idea of having a certificate for a nursing qualification, rather than a degree initially was all from the British colonial system. Nursing was never considered a profession in the first place but rather a vocation. Hence, a degree programme was not thought to be correct or necessary for acquiring a nursing qualification. Rather, it was something like 'one's calling' perhaps, initially not aknowledged by any formal certification but later attributed a certificate.

Thankfully, that soon changed. Coming here gave me the opportunity to return to university, albeit part time, whilst I was working. The fact is, I had that opportunity and consequently soon realised my dream of obtaining a first degree within the first few years of arriving in the UK. I look back and I think about the days when I had thought, "Oh I'd love to have a degree", just knowing that I had the ability and thinking that it would be something nice to write beside my name along with my nursing and midwifery qualifications. It seemed elusive at some points; however, I've never been in any doubt that it was something that was well within my grasp, and as soon as I had the opportunity, I took it with both hands. That to me is a version of success.

I was initially flabbergasted at the reticent attitudes I observed amongst many British citizens. To me, there were so many opportunities, so much to take, so much to embrace… and yet these golden nuggets of blessings seemed to be disregarded in many instances. I now know that the younger generation view their career routes in much less of a traditional way than my generation did. Many choose alternate pathways to achieving their career aspirations, e.g., apprenticeships, joining a franchise, becoming self-employed. I think these routes are great if they are what suit the individual. Moreover, in many instances these routes make much better financial sense.

However, it is vital that learning is continued when such pathways are chosen, even if not a formal educational course. Education is always key to ongoing development. I am very cognizant of the fact that success is not totally dependent on one's formal educational achievements, certainly not in our current digital, worldwide climate. However, for me, the route of traditional, formal education is what has worked for me and will be the route I embrace to allow the best chance of a successful and

Chapter 11

stable career. The benefits system in the UK also baffled me when I first learnt about it. How was it possible to get paid when you did not work? I found it incredulous that some individuals choose to stay home and not work when they probably could. I understand circumstances where people are genuinely unable to work and I think it is brilliant that there is a social security system that people can rely on.

I once heard a great quote that said, "We judge the civilisation of a society by how it cares for its vulnerable and older citizens". I truly embrace that ethos. It is remarkable that if someone is in need, whether it is because such an individual has fallen on hard times or for other reasons, that such a person is supported.

It is particularly comforting, if such individuals had, when they could have, contributed to society. However, I just could not grasp the perception of people deciding not to take up what seems to be the plethora of opportunities that were available to anyone and everyone, particularly those with British citizen status. Since my mindset was different, I embraced the opportunity to get my degree and boy, am I grateful!

Similarly, the National Health Service (NHS) is marvellous. It provided me with the opportunity to work as a staff nurse to enhance my profession in an environment that is highly acclaimed, highly systematised and highly structural. It is, dare I say, very bureaucratic sometimes but certainly a place that facilitates learning and climbing the career ladder, even if one must please individuals whom you would rather disagree with or drive a very hard bargain in negotiating one's way up. In my experience it allows and facilitates progression, for the most part.

I am not negating my input in bringing to fruition the achievements that I have managed to achieve within the NHS as some may argue that it was all down to my attitude and not the institution. However, the truth is that the facilities were provided in / by the NHS to encourage a desire and the motivation to achieve. For example, the bursary that was provided during my medical training was not enough to replace my G grade nurse's salary; however, it provided a route to help me at least get on the first rung of the ladder to becoming a doctor.

With this provision in place, my basic needs would be met. It meant that I had to find ways of providing for my other needs, but one has to agree that that bursary was a sound incentive. There may be 'cons' to this system, which if pressed, I could talk about. However, I strongly believe that the pros outweigh these, and I am still grateful that such an amazing opportunity existed within the NHS. I am truly grateful for the help that that afforded me as

Chapter 11

an individual but also as a woman. I hope that many other women have been able to realise their full potential with similar support systems that I believe may be available in various public sectors or industries in England.

I am aware of individuals who have not necessarily completed tertiary education in Jamaica and other developing countries, for the primary reason of a lack of a relevant support system. This is not to say that people should make excuses for apathy. However, there are authentic examples of individuals who possess brilliant minds and attitudes who were not supported to realise their full potential. A case in point, for me, was the lack of a support system at primary school or secondary school level in Jamaica.

Had I had a robust support system in place, I am in no doubt that I would have conquered the first hurdle of passing my Common Entrance Examination in Jamaica and may have mangaed to be a Spelling Bee champion, or at least, performed better than I did then. I reiterate these examples not to labour the point but to highlight the importance of good and relevant support systems in place, anywhere.

Growing up in Jamaica, I had a four-day primary school week. Going to primary school on a Friday was a luxury for us in my family. Fridays were the days when you helped in the field to get the provisions ready to get those products to the market on Saturday - not go to school! So, we made the best of the four days that we went to school, i.e., Monday to Thursday. The teachers knew that on Fridays only a handful of students were present in the class but I certainly do not think they had the resources to do anything about improving that. Rather, it was accepted and perhaps a welcome relief for the often-overcrowded classrooms. This is just a thought – my opinion!

One could argue that in the grand scheme of things this did not make a big difference. Perhaps, an argument could be put forward that the time spent on a Friday in the field was another form of education which gave me practical life skills which have helped me to succeed in other ways. This is an acceptable argument and one may never know what the reality is.

However, I found another way, and thank God, things turned out OK in the end. Nonetheless, I do believe that my experience as an adult is testament to the fact that support systems in place make all the difference or can make all the difference for an individual achieving success.

At medical school, if I or anyone was falling behind for any reason, there were support systems in place. For example, there were always extra study

Chapter 11

sessions, there were personal tutors whom one could always discuss things with and there was a pastoral system in place where non-academic matters which were impacting on one's education could be dealt with. I made use of all of those and thankfully got through medical school in the recommended period, without the need to repeat a year or re-sit final examinations. Similarly, in the GP training system there were lots of support systems in place, including the structured classes with educational tutors or clinical tutors and other extras.

It could be argued that the system itself generated several difficulties that might have otherwise been avoided: for example, the nature of the final GP exams is deemed notoriously flawed. And perhaps, a different method of assessing qualified doctors who have come to the end of three years' training in the GP training course could be more pragmatic and could potentially save the system many resources including funds used in various other ways. For example, the final GP clinical assessments have a lot of cultural influences in the actual exams.

For doctors who were not born or raised in England, they pose certain challenges. Arguably, these are not ones that pose a problem in real life, though they may contribute to a smoother consultation – for instance, my earlier reference to the array of variation in the everyday language that is used in England, which is not standard English. Although colloquialism is not used by the 'patient actors' in the exam, attitudes, demeanours and nuances of the culture are subtly incorporated. This is not about doctors who do not speak English as a first language and who need to pass a formal English language test; that is an entirely different scenario.

It is true that having a good grasp of formal English is integral to assimilating successfully into the culture; but a grasp of the social norms and mores is also crucial, as my experiences relayed earlier demonstrated. However, this is true of any country and culture and not unique to England.

Thankfully, my practical experiences of caring for patients were not hampered by this. In some cases, I have had to fight and work harder than others might have done but the outcome was the desired end. I am truly grateful to these wonderful individuals and institutions that supported me to achieve what I set out to achieve, what I dared to dream and to make those a reality for me.

You see, I believe that I can do all things, but it is always through Christ and I believe God has provided those resources for me. So, with all these things in place, why couldn't I possibly have it all? Can't I have it all? Of course, I can have it all; can't I really?

Chapter 11

After qualifying as a GP, earning handsomely, it is time to support my husband to get his elusive degree. Our lives have been total contrasts: I grew up in rural Jamaica, whereas he grew up pretty much in a life of luxury. However, he was late in achieving some of his goals.

Again, probably because of what I spoke about earlier where when things are handed to individuals on a plate, as it were, sometimes people do not embrace it as they should and perhaps that was one of the reasons for him not achieving and not having a degree up until that point. But I knew he was more than capable and by that time he was very motivated and keen to return to university to fulfil that dream. Moreover, at that time he knew exactly what he wanted to study and I was grateful that I was able to support him to do that.

So, my husband returned to university and for six years studied and emerged successfully with a master's degree in chemical engineering. That required a significant input and effort on my part to support the family singlehandedly for those six years but I was more than happy to do that because he had supported me throughout medical school, not necessarily financially but emotionally, despite our difficulties, and certainly when it came to looking after the children, he was fully present. Hence, now it was my turn to help – "I am at your service; I have no qualms in helping." After all we were a pair, a couple: we were going to conquer this world together and so why wouldn't I help? ...and that is exactly what I did!

During all of this, my children were also being schooled privately. It was hard work to able to finance all of that, but again, I felt it was doing what was best for my children, what was best for my family. My mindset was that if you can influence having the best family why wouldn't you?

It meant doing extra shifts but it was doing a job that I was proud of - being a doctor and I was enjoying doing it. Although it was taxing, in my capacity as a GP, I was reaping the benefit of being able to work in a flexible pattern that was much more suitable to me. So here I was doing my bit to make sure that my family was supported to be the best that it could be. This was to ensure that I had the best family unit that there could be. I recognised that in 'having it all', a strong family unit is of utmost importance!

Chapter 11

"It is crucial that you pause periodically to evaluate your journey and your progress. You will find there is always something to be grateful for."

Chapter 12

Have I Got it All?

Just over three years ago, I took stock, and if I had written it all down then, these were my thoughts: Surely, at this point I have got it all! At least, according to society's norms.

Now I am a qualified GP, I am earning handsomely - can easily make a 'six-figure' salary if I choose to. My husband has now got a matching qualification – a master's degree in chemical engineering. He could get a job with equally good remuneration. What more could a girl ask for?

Moreover, the children are in private boarding school. They are doing well and even if sometimes they complain, we believe they have got the best. They are being exposed to the best education that is available in this country; receiving the best stimulation and intermingling with the brightest minds, including other students not just from England but from an international community. These include children of world leaders and of renowned successful business owners.

I pause here to highlight an observation. Social status is an enduring topic that many are reluctant to engage with. In my experience, the British people

Chapter 12

have a peculiar relationship with being successful or wealthy. For example, I have never been able to understand why, in the UK, it is often seen as something to be ashamed of if one has attended a private fee-paying school (also referred to as a Public or Independent school in the UK). It is fascinating to listen to politicians badgering each other and judging who is the better person, based on who attended which school.

Persons who attend private schools are deemed to be less able to identify with the public, hence, a poorer political representative in comparison to their counterpart who attended state school. There are pros and cons but it seems to be a great big badge of honour just not having attended a private school, if you are a UK political leader. The reality is that many of our political leaders have attended private schools.

Statistics show that almost half of our modern British Prime Ministers attended Oxford University and, fewer, Cambridge. Only a handful attended state schools, with most having had a private education of some description. Some are even of aristocratic descent. It therefore seems a bit disingenuous for such a prevailing attitude to seemingly exist amongst the population.

In my opinion, this is opposite to the general attitude in Jamaica where it is a given that parents who can afford it will send their children to private (preparatory) schools to gift them with the best foundation education opportunity available. This is seen as commendable.

I have also observed a peculiarity in the general attitude of the UK public towards certain individuals who have worked hard and done well and made a name for themselves. Some people seem to thrive on calling them the most horrible names, criticising them for what I consider to be unfair and unnecessary reasons, simply because they and or their partners have done well.

I understand when people have gripes about the absolute unfairness surrounding pay structures, e.g., a footballer's salary, in comparison to that of a doctor, but the truth is, not many people seem to care about that, as the society is so 'football oriented'. On the other hand, I have personally been in a room when someone openly criticised GPs for the salary they make – not for service provision or anything else... just because of the money that they are able to make by way of running a GP surgery and or doing locum shifts or contracting their services independently.

I found that hurtful. When I think of someone like me, being in a certain income bracket, only because of the sheer amount of grafting and absolute hard

Chapter 12

work that I have put in, it totally baffles me, and I am still trying to understand such a mindset!

I consider myself to be part of middle England and I am not ashamed to say that. I care about the way my children speak, for example. If I were living in Jamaica, my children would speak 'proper English' and have a certain deportment. I do not see why it should be any different in England.

The dynamics in England, however, are double-edged: my boys may have felt that they did not fit in with the predominantly white community who were their peers at school and actively did things, including the way they spoke, dressed, and acted, to reinforce their difference. This created a dilemma for all the adults concerned. We have had issues at school when hairstyles they wished to have (afro or cornrows) and items of clothing they wore, like a hooded jumper were an issue. The truth is, as an individual with my Jamaican Christian background, certain aspects of popular culture, be it black or otherwise, do not appeal to me. However, I am a middle-aged woman (gorgeous one!) with a slightly different perspective from teenage black boys or young adult men growing up in England.

Moreover, these boys happen to be able to think independently and critically appraise arguments or social constructs. They also happen to be very aware of social justice, racial issues and feel quite strongly about justice and fairness. This, indeed, is a new challenge for my negotiation. I cannot say it is one that was not anticipated; issues like these become inevitable with children. Moreover, there is a particular uniqueness about being me and being my children.

We took the decision to send the children to private school not just because I want to fork out thousands of pounds every year, in fact every month, but because we want them to have the best. I do not want them to end up being 'statistics'. The issues that black boys encounter in this country are real. There is robust evidence that black boys, particularly those with a black Caribbean heritage, fare worse in the British state education system.

For me this was not just theoretical, it wasn't just research findings or something I heard on the news, it was the reality of what I saw could have happened to my own children. I believe that some of the issues relating to the educational system are partly to do with the fact that the state schools are not always equipped with all the resources that are needed to deal with children from different cultural heritages and also to deal with children who learn differently.

My sons certainly learned differently and in certain ways they were treated differently. Certainly, the older one was deemed to be "too lively" from an early age at nursery. But what do our nursery nurses

Chapter 12

and teachers in England do with that observation or information that may be passed on? Unfortunately, it is often just used as a label rather than an opportunity to explore such a child's unique learning style and often to the detriment of the child's educational experience.

There is evidence to indicate that more black children, like mine, are excluded from mainstream education simply because of behaviour patterns. Children like those "lively" ones are deemed to be misfits. It would appear that the support systems that should be in place at this stage of the educational infrastructure are not available or are not being appropriately implemented. On the other hand, is this merely evidence of a deficient state-funded educational system?

We have had to find ways of ensuring that whatever or whoever our children were being educated or influenced by; whatever deficiencies or deficits they may have had would not prevent them from achieving their maximum potential. This was the reality and the true driver for the educational pathway that we chose for them.

We felt it was necessary to make that investment to put them in an environment where their learning expressions and different learning styles could be catered to. An environment where, hopefully, their differences would not be looked at as something to be quashed and a label to be used against them. Rather, their difference would be embraced and they would be encouraged to express themselves in suitable ways, facilitating their full development so that they could be the best children that they could possibly be. Our parental input by being good examples and affording our children our time was also integral. My children themselves and time will be the best judges as to whether that was achieved. However, I can say, that we tried. Was it our best? We did the best we knew.

So, the children are being taken care of. What next to 'having it all'? A lovely house and home. It so happened, that this home is in a location near to our local church – an absolute bonus!

The spacious nature and layout of the house have facilitated an easier maintenance, as such it is easier to keep tidy and welcoming. It is a haven for me and my family and not just my immediate family but for my extended family to visit and for us to have quality time with each other. Everyone agrees, appreciates and enjoys the attributes of this house and the pleasures it allows in our home.

When we first moved into this house, my husband reminisced and expressed a feeling of it "being all worth it", particularly, when we shared with all our nearest and dearest as we hosted the celebrations of Christmas 2017. When we lived in

Chapter 12

our previous house which was smaller, I always told myself that this house is lovely, and it served the purpose for then, but I'd love something better. I made every effort to look after that house to the best of my ability, paying for it to be cleaned professionally once a fortnight, when I could not physically afford the time to do so.

This was especially so during the days of medical school when I was overwhelmed with doing what then was most important - trying to get through medical school but also it was important to maintain a clean, healthy, and relaxing home environment and for that I was willing to part with some of my limited funds. This is still very important to me. I always subscribe to the principle that if we look after what God has given to us, as good stewards, then God can trust us with greater things.

I would make it a point of duty, e.g., to look after the front garden because that was my designated area of responsibility. Living in my current home is no different. I have no hesitations about allocating funds for someone to assist me in creating the optimum living environment.

For me, a good home environment is crucial to my success, and I actively pay attention to creating that. The assistance others provide me with in this area is never seen or taken lightly and ties into my earlier discourse about needing others in our lives to succeed. Our angels come in the form of different people to fulfil various roles in our lives as well as theirs. With all this in place, I was truly grateful. I really felt a sense of fulfilment and it really seemed, at this point, that finally, I was beginning to have it all. Even my car was better! I had now traded my old £500 'run around' for a nice top brand SUV vehicle which I thoroughly enjoy driving, even if driving it was all I did! I later realised I did not even know how to open the car bonnet!

This is hilarious but, hey, a clear demonstration of faith, I say. "You don't have to understand how it works to use it as long as you know it will deliver when you need it to." This is akin to my relationship with God and the lack of explanation or answers that I am sometimes able to provide when faced with questions about my Christian faith, either from myself or others. "I don't always have the answers, but I know it (my relationship with Jesus Christ) works!"

Our life's trajectory is a progressive one and just as how I was forced to learn to open the car bonnet, by circumstances, i.e., when I desperately needed screen wash poured in so my windscreen would be clean for me to see clearly to drive safely; sometimes, life's circumstances force us to learn what is necessary. As a Christian, this often means an opportunity to foster a closer relationship with my God where I study His word more intently,

Chapter 12

subsequently, learning and understanding more about Him and His guiding principles, therefore, becoming more enlightened. The spiritual aspect of my life is tremendously important to me. My spiritual growth is crucial.

I endeavour not just to work to earn money, but to serve. Practically, this means striving to do whatever I can in a community setting to show gratitude and love to God and others around me. In fulfilling these goals, I serve in several voluntary roles, e.g., in my local church, which is also a registered charity, and assisting other charities and community groups particularly in health promotion.

Periodically I assist some of my older friends who are housebound by providing them with a home-cooked meal in a quest to ensure that these individuals are also looked after.

I highlight these things because sometimes we are reluctant to put ourselves forward for what seems like inconsequential roles. However, there is much to be gained, personally and from a community and societal stance by availing ourselves to such roles.

Loneliness in the elderly is now known to be an independent risk factor for dying and is undoubtedly a significant contributor to poor mental health, in general. A simple act of kindness, e.g., bringing a home-cooked meal for individuals, especially those of ethnic minority backgrounds, is often very much appreciated. This is particularly relevant as many of these older individuals often struggle to access the food that they are accustomed to eating and enjoy, for various reasons. They are often forced to eat meals that they do not particularly enjoy and would not have otherwise eaten but do so only as a means of surviving.

I do not consider this a luxury to be able to eat and enjoy the food that one has always enjoyed, particularly in one's later years. I would like lots of nice Jamaican food when I am older; wouldn't you like to enjoy your native food or the food that you enjoy most, when you are older?

In giving educational talks via various forums, I aim to empower individuals with knowledge about their health and the need to embrace holistic health. With this in mind, I also serve others by supporting organisations, like the British Heart Foundation, as heart health has become one of my greatest passions. I also offer advice in forums for younger people, such as in career advice forums.

My family relationship has always been fundamental to my success and I consider having sound relationships all round as integral to being successful. I am often told of conversations with individuals in their later years or at the end of their lives; invariably, it is the relationship that was sacrificed or never maximized that people mourn. It is not the additional money they did not earn or the material possession they did not acquire. Forging great relationships is non-negotiable for me and I am grateful for the amazing individuals in my life.

In continuing the discourse about success and managing crisis and contemplating whether I have it all, there is also an important viewpoint which I hold that is worth discussing. This outlook may surprise or even shock some individuals, especially those with a secular perspective. There is no doubt that I describe myself as a fiercely independent woman who has a brain that she uses to think for herself and holds several leadership roles. In addition, I know who and what I am. I do not have an identity issue – that is success in itself! Nevertheless, I subscribe to the biblical teaching of submission.

According to the Bible, women are encouraged to be submissive to their husbands. Many people frown on that and see it as a bad thing which is not congruent with the thinking of a modern, progressive and successful woman.

However, the Bible actually teaches mutual, rather than unilateral submission. The Bible also teaches that men ought to love their wives as Christ loves the church (Ephesians 5:21-31). If you think about it, Christ loved the church so much that he gave his life for it. When I speak about the church, I am referring to the called-out group of individuals (ecclesia) who have accepted Christ as their personal Lord and Saviour, then continue an ongoing relationship with Him. In fact, Christ gave his life for us even before we became the church (St John 3:16) but as the church, we are likened to as His bride.

A bride that He paid the highest possible price for; whom he loves and adores; whom he nourishes and cares for delicately; protects and provides for and will stop at nothing to ensure she fulfils her ultimate potential. Christ will return for this bride to be with him eternally in His position as king. This bride will not just be with him in any redundant or passive way but will REIGN with him.

This is a picture of equality in essence but demonstrating a functional hierarchy. Ultimately, this bride will share in His eternal glory – they both shine! So, in my view, there is nothing wrong with me as a wife, submitting to such a husband. If my husband is willing to do all of the aforementioned for me, certainly I do not have a problem submitting because it does not relegate me to a lower status or to be the one without a voice.

There is nothing in that concept that suggests that one person is worth more than the other; it is simply denoting a system of order and function. To be

Chapter 12

honest, as a woman I am not bothered about having the burden of family responsibilities. I am willing to do my part but ultimately, I prefer my husband to be the one to have the responsibility for looking after me and my children. I want him to be the one to shoulder that responsibility.

I want to be loved and pampered, cared for, nourished, treasured, protected, and provided for, even if I am capable of this independently. It's the woman in me that I make no apologies about. You can guarantee that if that is the case, I will always shine and reciprocate in my own unique way! To me, submission is about having the discipline to control and mange one's power or authority, because a powerful force or weapon used indiscriminately can cause utter destruction.

Someone once said, "An organism with two heads is a monster." Being a successful woman certainly does not, for me, involve being at loggerheads with my husband to assume a leadership role in the household or in our relationship. Rather, I expect such leadership from my husband in order to have a successful relationship and family life.

"Success means being wholly fulfilled in all facets of your life – body, soul and spirit. Underpinning this is the mastery of forging and maintaining sound relationships all round. And, by the way, 'submission' is not a bad word!"

Chapter 13

Myocardial Infarction (Heart Attack) Crisis

Talk about crisis. I have been through quite a few but I have also achieved quite a lot. If you ask me, I will say, "That's life!". Life gives and life takes; life is composed of seasons and none of us can escape. I have just, in the previous chapter, described how beautiful life is and how contented I am and how everything has finally fallen into place. I even expressed the fact that, maybe I had finally got it all together, after all!

Should I be surprised to know that there was something else lurking around the corner? Something that I could not have imagined in a million years. Something that had not 'graced' my thoughts. Something that I would have never attributed to myself, because, according to conventional wisdom, it was almost impossible. There were no signs, no known risk factors, nothing to suggest that that could possibly be an issue to even contemplate.

However, whether I like it or not, here I am reminiscing about how, at the age of 48, Carol S. Douglas Ighofose experienced a heart attack. These words continue to sound strange; they just do not sound real; they do not seem to be synonymous with me. I look back on that day and ponder how my life might have been snuffed out of me in seconds! Nevertheless, I am here to tell the story and I am grateful; truly grateful to God for having kept me alive. I am also grateful that I have had the courage to deal with it and here I am today, doing my best and endeavouring to deal with the aftermath of this totally unexpected event – an acclaimed major life crisis and make the best of my experience.

I recently learnt that Dr Caroline Leaf, a cognitive neuroscientist, describes this approach that I have instinctively adopted to this trauma as 'reconceptualizing'. I have written extensively about my experience of having a heart attack in my first book, entitled, **Fearfully and Wonderfully Made: The HEART of the Matter!** (Subtitled: Why Heart Attacks Happen and a Plan for Living Well after the Event). Chronicling my experience proved to be very cathartic at the time. My account has served as a source of enlightenment, encouragement, and empowerment for many, particularly as I wrote from the perspective of being a medical doctor having a patient's experience.

Three years on, I look back, having been contemplating the real reasons for my heart attack. As alluded to earlier, I did not possess the conventional risk factors that would immediately be recognised as the reasons for such a well-studied and relatively well understood pathology. However,

Chapter 13

in retrospect and with increased clarity of thought, I have been able to list what I feel were risk factors that were staring me in the face but in the face of which either I had buried my head in the sand or I had just not paid enough attention because they were not the conventional ones that I would 'plug' into my 'Q-Risk' calculator three years ago.

Based on the known risk factors for a heart attack, I came out with 'flying colours', that is with a very low percentage risk of having such an ischaemic event at that time in my life. In fact, based on my apparent health status at that time, the 'calculator' advised that I could expect to live well into my eighties without experiencing such events as a heart attack or a stroke.

My crisis event has simply revealed, even clearer, that we know a lot about heart attacks and strokes but not everything and that, sometimes, we need a more honest, heart-to-heart discussion about what is really happening in our lives; about what is really bothering us; about what is really eating us versus what we are eating, rather than the superficial discussions that we usually have.

Often, our discussions are not deep because that is what we have time for or because we are too polite to probe deeply and unearth real issues in our friends, family or even in our patients, for those of us who function as healthcare professionals. Many times, our focus is to avoid upsetting the apple cart. However, in some cases, it is the case that all concerned have been genuinely blind-sided! I now recognise factors that I thought I had done enough to remedy, but perhaps had only covered with a sticking plaster. It seemed the damage had already been done - well, obviously! The crisis was inevitable. The structure and integrity of my precious left anterior descending artery (LAD) had been pathologically changed forever, without my having any knowledge about it.

That plaque had formed in my artery, over a period, who knows for how long - I had been without symptoms! But there came a time on that day, the 22nd of January 2018, when for whatever reason that plaque ruptured, releasing its thrombogenic core into the lumen of my LAD artery. My body responded as expected, by forming a clot to curb the injury. Unfortunately, a clot forming in an artery is bad news, despite the body's best intentions.

The result was certain blockage, restricting and eventually cutting off the blood supply to the area of my heart muscle that was being perfused by my LAD artery causing a total lack of blood supply (ischaemia) initially and eventually caused infarction (death) of the affected area of heart muscle, that is, a large area to the front of my left ventricle. This rendered that portion of my heart

Chapter 13

muscle changed forever in its make-up and function. An unexpected and major crisis indeed! Thank God I survived the ordeal - but what really caused it?

The true answer is that I or my doctors may never truly know. The conventional risk factors for heart attacks include male sex, older age, genetics and family history, obesity, and poor lifestyle factors including smoking, excessive alcohol intake and inactivity. High cholesterol levels, previous heart attack, diabetes, hypertension and mental illness are also known risk factors.

Stress is not deemed an independent risk factor but an association, which indirectly causes heart attack through poor lifestyle choices. Other risk factors now being highlighted include air pollution, Vitamin D deficiency and poor oral health. In 2018, I was not known to possess any of the above risk factors, hence my previous assertion that I did not have any of the conventional risk factors at the time of having a heart attack.

However, with retrospective analysis and having investigated my family history further, I have identified the following as possible risk factors. I believe it is important that I did this and also keen to share my thoughts as the quest for success involves being willing to investigate, introspect, analyse and acknowledge problems and make changes to remedy existing problems or to prevent similar ones occurring in the future.

    1.   Unknown genetic mutation. This has not been identified to date and I believe is less likely to be the case. However, as that factor has still not been ruled out definitively, I am unable to confidently say it is not a factor for me. Following the heart attack, I learnt that my maternal grandfather died of a heart attack at the age of 46! The information surrounding this is limited as I do not have additional information to substantiate this being the result of a genetic problem.

The common genetic disorders that would be most likely to cause such early cardiac death include familial hypercholesterolaemia, cardiac arrythmias or hypertrophic cardiomyopathy (HOCM). I do not have any of the above conditions and as far as I have been advised, no close member of my family suffers from these conditions, suggesting that these conditions do not 'run in the family'.

It is very possible that my grandfather's early demise from a heart attack may have been related to his lifestyle choices or other environmental factors, rather than genetics. However, that is unknown.

Chapter 13

2. Impact from subclinical conditions including episodes of pregnancy-induced hypertension (PIH) and being at risk for T2DM. A recorded HBA1c of 6.1% is documented in my medical records. Following the heart attack, my HBA1c spiked dramatically but settled later. This is a common stress response by the body in events such as a heart attack but is worth keeping a close eye on. However, I have not met the criteria to be diagnosed with diabetes, not even during pregnancy, although I am currently labelled as 'at risk'.

With a strong family history of diabetes in second-generation relatives, I am treating this as a potential risk factor that may have contributed. My blood pressure returned to normal after both pregnancies. However, I have a first-generation relative, my father, with hypertension, which increases my risk. The knowledge about being at risk for these two conditions that increases individuals' risk of cardiovascular diseases (CVD) including heart attacks and strokes, has always inspired me to make good lifestyle choices, to do what lies in my power to minimise the risk of developing the conditions.

I have had investigations for other pro-inflammatory markers, such as a raised homocysteine level which may have predisposed my arteries to an earlier than usual atherosclerotic process, but these were all negative.

3. Stress. I firmly believe that the effects of stress were significant contributors to my having a heart attack. As I stated above, stress is not listed as an independent risk factor but there is substantial evidence from observational studies to show a direct correlation, rather than a mere indirect relationship, such as from associated poor lifestyle choices.

   For example, there are changes that occur in the amygdala of the brain and in the functioning of our hypothalamic-pituitary-adrenal (HPA) axis that influence adverse changes in the rest of our body, including inflammatory responses that could cause physical changes in our blood vessels associated with heart attacks. (Additional details on this may be obtained from my first book, available on Amazon or via www.carolighofose.com.)

   The things that I was very much aware of as personal stressors include my hectic work pattern and the nature of my job. Being a doctor requires making significant decisions several times a day which impact upon other individuals' lives; in some cases a decision

Chapter 13

may be the difference between life and death. Hence it is a stressful situation to be in on an almost daily basis and on many occasions, for several hours per day. Nevertheless, this does not have to result in catastrophic events such as heart attacks. What it points to is the importance of acknowledging and managing our stress.

One thing that I may have underestimated is also the effect of the circumstances and dynamics in my family life that I was constantly negotiating, especially in earlier years, some of which I have alluded to in this book. I dealt with those to the best of my ability and felt satisfied to move forward, just managing eventualities as they occurred. However, it appears the effects were greater than I was willing to admit.

4. Poor sleep pattern. Sleep is underestimated. I have heard statements like, "Lack of sleep kills no-one", or "Sleep is overrated; it just stops us from getting on with things that we need to do." These statements came from highly-motivated professionals or other individuals who felt that there was not enough time in the day to accomplish what they needed to. I dare say that such remarks signify both ignorance and arrogance. The ignorant individual lacks knowledge on the

effects of sleep, such as the effects it has on our telomeres, the pro-inflammatory process that it fosters and the way it changes our body's response to food desired or craved, via the hormones - ghrelin and leptin.

This phenomenon increases our latent predispositions to chronic diseases, such as hypertension and diabetes, listed above, particularly because of how our body may handle the increased energy intake, resulting in obesity.

It is also worth noting that studies have shown an increased incidence of heart attacks during daylight-saving time when the clocks are moved forward, causing us to lose one hour of sleep, compared to fewer incidents when the clocks are moved back! Who would have thought? The World Health Organisation (WHO) has also listed sleep disruption from shift work as a probable carcinogen, that is, a possible risk factor for developing cancer. Sleep deprivation also causes changes in our cognitive function and increases our sensitivity to pain.

Arrogance is demonstrated when individuals brag about the number of hours they work, equating it to superior efforts and motivation. Such individuals, I have found, tend to 'look down' on

Chapter 13

individuals who require more sleep, e.g., eight hours or more each night (which is healthy and necessary for most individuals). Personally, I have always had a weird sleep pattern: perhaps it stems from the days when I had to make necessary adjustments to navigate waking up early – like at 4am, to get the bus to school, and sometimes getting to bed quite late for various reasons, including getting home late or having to stay up late to complete assignments for the following school day.

Especially if I did not manage to complete them in the bus on my journey home from school! I tend to be able to sleep comfortably for only four hours at a time. This does not mean that that is all the sleep I require, but I am able to function quite well on four hours' sleep but can return to bed at any time to 'catch up' on my sleep.

Research has shown that this is not necessarily the best sleep pattern as a lot of emphasis is placed on regularity in one's sleep pattern. Regularity has been shown to have superior outcomes on individual's health. My opportunity for a more consistent sleep pattern improved when I gave up shift work and stopped doing my marathon 12-hour night shifts. However, old habits die hard and this is an area that I am still working towards improving.

5. Relaxation. I had recognised the need for this and had started to set aside a 'relaxation day'

to foster recuperation after each week of very hectic work. I would go swimming on those days, but even that could be stressful at times, getting across town to the nice gym that I wanted to use. I would sit in front of the TV on returning home from a tough day as my way of 'winding down' but would feel guilty for doing so because of comments that I had inadvertently internalised.

On many occasions, when we took a family break, I would, of necessity only partially enjoy them as I would almost certainly spend half of it doing locum shifts – which I was happy to do at the time. My justification was that I was doing it for my family to ensure that we could reap the benefits later when we did not have the expenses we had then and could enjoy more 'proper' and truly luxurious holidays. I cannot stress the importance of deliberate and timed relaxation periods NOW, even if it is for a few minutes each day.

So, I have survived, and I have been able to reminisce and analyse, even if it is retrospectively, what real factors may have led to my experience of encountering such a major unexpected life crisis. My physical health has been impacted permanently, e.g., my ejection fraction which is the percentage of blood that the heart is able to eject with each beat seems to

Chapter 13

be now stabilised around 35%, versus 18% immediately after the heart attack. Around 65 - 70% is necessary for the heart adequately to perfuse all the tissues in the body from the brain to the toes.

The impact is that I do struggle with fatigue. I get tired, particularly towards the end of the day. However, I am grateful that I do not have many physical symptoms such as shortness of breath, excessive swelling of legs/other body parts from fluid collection (oedema) or palpitations. I hope that those signs and symptoms of heart failure will not come to fruition. Nevertheless, it means taking daily doses of several tablets which sometimes is a bit of a nuisance.

It is also worth mentioning here that one cannot escape the psychological impact of a heart attack - and I am no exception. This is difficult and requires time to get over what happened and the possible impact that the event has had on me. There is the impact on my finances as well as on my relationships and the way I now perceive myself. Am I any less of a person? Do I trust my body or do I feel it has let me down despite my best efforts? How about my relationship with God - has this affected my faith? How? These are questions that I am still negotiating and, in a quest to answer the question about success and managing life's crises - did I or have I got it all? Can I ever?

"When aspects of your life remain out of sync; it will inevitably be manifested. Sometimes this is dramatically demonstrated in surprising and unconventional ways that may catch us totally unaware!"

Chapter 14

So, what then is success?

How is success decided or defined?

I seem to have had it all; it seems I had made a success of my life by any standards! Of course, I will hasten to say, as always, I did it through Christ's strength. Having had the resilience and the courage to travel to and live in different countries and to have withstood, bypassed or climbed the obstacles that were placed in my way, I had been able to overcome much.

Today, having the things that I possess, being able to function physically, intellectually, spiritually, emotionally and having a reasonable quality of life, despite all the ills - isn't that success? It can be argued that success is dependent on one's outlook, and hence the concept means different things to different people. For some, success is defined by one's achievements and physical possessions, including education, job or career position, house and money. For some, success is defined by the state of their health, while others use the state of their relationships as a yardstick.

For some, being successful and wealthy are synonymous, whilst for others wealth, success and riches are all different things. For me, success looks like being the best version of oneself – body, soul and spirit. This outlook acknowledges the need for balance in one's life to claim or declare success. This is predicated on the reality that we are not merely physical beings but are essentially tripartite beings.

It is about having a strategy or framework in place to deal with life's eventualities and executing the most appropriate actions at the right time. How one views situations, the methods used to analyse or scrutinise an actual, perceived or anticipated problem and the actions taken when faced with these situations can make all the difference for the eventual outcome. Having acquired the status of being a registered nurse, a midwife, a wife, a mother, a doctor, an author, a speaker, a missionary and by extension, a leader in my community, do I consider myself to be successful today? Yes, I do. I do because I have made the best of what I have been given. It is possible that, as an individual, I could have done more.

For instance, I did not stick with learning to play a musical instrument – something I still yearn to do but feel like now is not the time to give that priority. However, I believe I made good use of available and or limited resources and maintained the correct mindset - and when the ball has been in my court I have taken a shot, usually with the mindset to win but knowing realistically, that it may be win or lose.

Chapter 14

For the most part, I have had winning shots, though there have, undoubtedly been some disappointing results too. One of my greatest observations, however, is that it appears that I have had to work sometimes twice as hard to win those shots. Nevertheless, the prospect of working hard will never be a deterrent! Not having tried would have been the true failure.

I have never believed for one second that the achievements I have attained have been realised only through my efforts. As I mentioned previously, my mantra is, "I can do all things through Christ who strengthens me" (Philippians 4:13).

This emphasises the concept of needing a greater power than oneself to achieve success. It is about understanding that you are empowered to achieve your dreams and desires but to guard against pride and self-indulgence. For me that greater power is Jesus Christ. I am also constantly reminded that I need others to thrive and to be successful. Therefore, it is important to surround ourselves with the right people who will love, encourage and support us and who we trust.

Being able to do all things through Christ may seem a controversial position for some people because if you can 'do' all things through Christ why can't you 'have' all things through Christ? What does that mean? The Bible verse is found in

Philippines 4:13. I spend my life quoting, believing, and drawing from this scripture. To look at it in a more analytical way this is how I see it: In every situation, I can do well because of my union with Christ. Our real enemy is Satan who promotes despair, fear, feelings of helplessness and disempowerment.

Though St Paul was in prison when he wrote this verse, his mindset was that of a conqueror! His was a victorious mindset. Things are constantly going wrong in life; there are always minor crises; not to mention the major ones, but we can overcome them empowered by Jesus Christ. According to the Word Biblical Commentary, Hawthorne and Martin, a more comprehensive translation is, "I have the power to face all such situations in union with the One who continually infuses me with strength." I really like that. For me, success is about having the confidence to make a decision based on what you know deep down is right for you. That is what gives you peace, what will help you to grow, to develop, to be able to express yourself freely.

It is about having the courage not to go along with the status quo but to be confident enough to choose what you deem to be the most suitable for you if the principles are in keeping with your core beliefs, e.g., your faith and your conscience. What does this look like in real life? It is about saying no to abuse, to being used, to unfounded traditions and

Chapter 14

legalisms, to say enough is enough, to be willing to part with what seems to be the thing that is supposed to give you that marker of acceptance and success in society if it's 'killing' you: that is, to be willing to be stripped of society's labels for success and to be willing to forge one's own path if that is what it takes. It is about having the courage to walk away from a job that is draining, unfulfilling and is clearly a "dead end" with no reasonable prospects. It is about being able to walk away from an abusive relationship - whatever form that may take.

I appreciate that some individuals, women in particular, do not have the luxury of the ability or the freedom to walk away from a home situation, for example where they do not have recourse to other forms of income. However, for me, even in such a situation, success is about being able to recognise an abusive environment, seeking help and planning an exit strategy whilst the opportunity still exists. My endeavours to give my children the very best have been a case in point. I also expected them to follow a certain pathway.

This has not necessarily been to dictate to them what to become in life, but I expect at least a generic pathway of traditional things such as finishing high school with good grades - especially having gone to a private secondary/high school - then going to university and choosing a career path with good career prospects. However, it does not seem to have been the case -certainly not where my older son is concerned. At secondary/high school he did very well to demonstrate himself as an extremely resilient individual. He had some difficult times but still managed to show his leadership skills and was elected as head of his boarding house.

That is quite a prestigious position in the circle of private boarding schools, and I was very touched that despite the challenges he encountered in that particular setting he had shown himself worthy. It is often very difficult for children of ethnic minority backgrounds who find themselves in predominantly white middle class settings to remain outstanding and not lose themselves. My boy had experienced individuals who had acted in unkind and unconventional ways towards him on numerous occasions. He had faced challenges that, perhaps, were unique to his position of being in the minority group in that community, but had triumphed.

Having triumphed socially and emotionally, his announcement that he had made the decision not to go to university following high school was unexpected. For me, that has been a difficult pill to swallow. That called into question how successful I have been in this quest to give my children the best. In fact, it made me seriously question not just how successful I have been as a mother but as an individual. Ultimately, we dream that our children's success and achievements will far outweigh ours. I

Chapter 14

certainly do! Given my background, it is about affording my children the basic things in life that I did not have access to, hoping that accessing those things would give them a significant head start, affording them every chance of success in life, in a way that I was not privileged to have.

In addition, I was determined that they would not be disadvantaged in comparison to most children in the UK, despite being an ethnic minority child of African-Caribbean descent.

However, I have concluded that another way to look at my son's decision is that I have raised a very independent young man who is able to stand independently on his feet, think outside the box and not be a slave to society's norms and even to what his parents seem to dictate. How dare you defy your parents, young man?

We are supposed to be intelligent, intellectual, professional people who know best! The path he has chosen does suit him: he is enjoying it, is thriving and even gaining experiences that I have not had in my conventional pathway. For example, his career path has allowed him to travel to exotic countries on business summits and conventions. I have not been to some of the places that he has been able to visit, and at least one of those countries. Hence I admire him for that and I can only vote to support him so that he can become that best version of himself as his marker of success. I am in constant dialogue with my younger son and waiting to see what he will choose to do. He too has very strong convictions, very strong feelings about right and wrong and a good sense of justice. My two Princes are strong characters and boy, they can defend themselves. I will continue to support them, pray for them and be there for them - being the best mother I can be.

I will encourage them, hoping and believing with everything that I have that they both will be successful - by which I mean to become the best version of themselves to support themselves and their families in a way that does not cause them undue stress and force them to live a life which is filled with drudgery. But rather, that they will be able to enjoy what they have been blessed with, what they have acquired through their work and, most of all, their relationships, because these are truly of ultimate importance! I think that success as a parent is having the courage to allow your children to flourish.

That means guiding them with what you know to be the best information, advice and being an example. I believe it is incumbent on parents to provide children with all the resources that you have the ability to provide and allowing the children to make guided and informed decisions. This is done in collaboration with educators and other

Chapter 14

individuals who happen to be influential in their lives. It is not easy, as a parent, to keep a tight rein whilst avoiding strangling your children especially if you feel that the path that they seem to be taking is not what you would have chosen.

It is having the courage constantly to reaffirm what you deem to be right but allowing them the freedom to choose the things that they are interested in, passionate about, are excelling at and are happy seamlessly to pursue. There is no denying that this takes guts. However, I think this underpins the character of a successful parent. I am a parent who also believes that having a personal relationship with Jesus Christ is a sure foundation upon which any person, young or otherwise, can build a superior life edifice. That is a prayer that I am constantly praying for my boys. My husband has also chosen an unconventional career path; he is doing things differently.

He tells me his dream is to become uber-successful in his entrepreneurial endeavours and show me yet a higher level of achievement! Time will reveal all… Unfortunately, we have not been able to continue our lives together as a couple. A high price for success I hear you say / ask. Remember, it's about your definition of success. Mine is about having the courage to do what it takes to achieve being the best version of myself. Nonetheless, the question rings true: "Can women have it all?" Could I have done anything differently? I am sure there are things that I could have done differently but would it have meant a better outcome? Who knows? Life happens and this is life. We don't get a trial run, but we do get opportunities to learn from our experiences and, perhaps, do things differently if presented with similar scenarios. To reiterate: Life is not straightforward. Life is not a straight trajectory.

It is filled with winding, undulating paths, unexpected turns, and sheer surprises such as I have experienced. Uncertainties, disappointments, bereavements, hard times, adversities, and drudgery in life are just purely part and parcel of life. They do not occur just because someone is out to get you or because someone has worked some 'magic' on you or because the demons are only after you. Such factors may be part of the mix, but crises happen, for the most part, because this is life in a fallen world.

Life is about acknowledging that failure is inevitable. However, success is about having the ability to ask oneself, "What is this here to teach me?" Having worked out, or even in the process of working out the answer to that question, it is about knowing that one may fall many times but that it is in getting up after every single fall and each time realising that you are that bit closer the next time around; that success will eventually be realised. Such a mindset and such actions will, undoubtedly,

Chapter 14

bring success, even if it takes a while. I recently heard someone say that if you set out for London and start on and remain on the correct road, even if some temporary detours become necessary, you will get to London eventually, even if it takes weeks, months or even years to arrive.

My life has not turned out to be this nicely-framed picture that I created in my head and hung perfectly on the wall of my life's living room. I have had to take it down and allowed a different drawing, a different compilation. It is still under construction; It is not necessarily the way I thought the picture would look, but boy, is it more interesting? You bet it is! Moreover, it is not just interesting but still beautiful - maybe even more beautiful than my original version. There are lots of variations that I would not have put in if it were left up to me alone. But, then my original picture would have arguably, been very boring; very mundane; very 'run of the mill' and all those other synonyms.

Certainly, the picture that is currently being drawn, being painted, is anything but a boring one. Those words are ill-placed to describe my new picture and that is exciting! That to me sounds like success. I am sure if I were to auction this version, it would fetch a higher price than the one that I was originally painting.

"Your definition of success must be a personal one, not what society dictates. It is, essentially, about being the best version of yourself at any given time."

Chapter 15

Can I really have it all?

What is "IT ALL"?

Is it health? Is it beauty? Is it wealth? Is it family? Is it career? Is it...? What is it? Is it a combination of all those things or is it just "that one thing" that is very important to you? That one thing that if you were to achieve it, you would consider your life worth it - that you would consider that having acquired or achieved that one thing means that you have been successful on this earth and that your life was worth living? So, let us analyse the concept a bit more.

Ask yourself this question: Could I as an individual have flawless beauty, complete health (physical, mental, emotional, and spiritual), the perfect family, impeccable relationships, the picture-perfect career, absolute wealth and the unblemished connection and fellowship with God – all at once?

Well, I do not know anybody who has the perfect 'all those things', especially concurrently! Do you? Furthermore, I do not know that it is possible for such a status to exist on this earth. I think we may be talking about Utopia here. So really, if that is the case then it is clear that no woman can have it all!

CAN WOMEN HAVE IT ALL?

But why does society expect so much from women, and what does society mean when it asserts that you can have it all? Or when they ask, can you have it all? Or when it pushes or forces you to think that you can and, indeed, must have it all? What, then, is society asking?

Let us bear in mind the background and origin of this concept as I outlined earlier in this book's introduction. The concept of "having it all" was made popular in the 1980's when Helen Gurley Brown, an accomplished editor of *Cosmopolitan* magazine and author of the renowned book *'Having It All: Love, Success, Sex, and Money...Even If You're Starting with Nothing'*, sought to share her strategy for success with an increasing demographic of single working women. The book essentially provided advice as to how ordinary women could make their way to the very top. Her approach was well received and served as an inspiration for many women to realise their dreams.

Today, the concept is predominantly used to describe a woman's journey of finding balance in her personal and professional life. 'Having it all' refers to securing success in career, raising children, maintaining sound relationships and contributing to the larger society whilst still finding time to take care of herself and looking and feeling at her best.

Chapter 15

It is important to understand that the things listed above that are valued by society, that society recognises as a statement of achievement or a statement of success, do not have to be your definition of success. My own experience and those voiced and documented by many like-minded women demonstrate that unfortunately, as one acquires each of those things, something else still appears to be amiss.

The truth is, you cannot possibly physically be that unblemished career woman who is at the top of her game, who is also looking after her home and her family perfectly by anyone's standard, including meeting her husband's and her children's various needs without any complaints from anyone. It is simply not possible. Furthermore, to enjoy the perfect career and home / family life and look after yourself so that you are meeting all YOUR needs as well, requires additional demands on you. Is that achievable?

You could argue that the solution would be to delegate some of the activities and have the time necessary to do the things that are important to you. However, would you then feel guilty that you are not this 'domestic goddess' that society invented? Would you feel guilty that your friend does the gardening and you don't? Would you then feel guilty that you are not necessarily the one washing and ironing your husband's and children's clothes and picking up the children from school or dropping them off? What would you feel guilty about then if you were not able to do everything?... and by God, you could not possibly do everything!

So, what would be the solution? I think if by having it all, we mean one woman being perfectly beautiful - always immaculately turned out with perfectly manicured nails, not a hair out of place (or, indeed, in place when it should not be), your husband never complaining because his wife is always there at his beck and call.

You are a woman who is fulfilled because she has achieved her intellectual heights; she knows she is intelligent and she has proven that to the world; she is not just seen as a 'stay-at-home' mum or rather the 'bitchy' heartless professional or career woman who leaves her children to the care and mercy of others. What then of her spiritual health? Does that feature? Will she serve in her church or relevant spiritual organisation, or in her local community and be always lacking at nothing with an intact conscience? If it is all of those, it is absolutely clear that a woman cannot have it all!

If "having it all" means achieving the best possible version of herself and enjoying and accepting that at any given time, then "Yes, she can have it all". If this is the consensus, then by my standard and accomplishments, I can 'have it all'. In

Chapter 15

addition, the same is also true by God's standard (see Philippians 4:13; Ephesians 3:20; 2 Corinthians 9:8; I Kings 3:13). However, I am clear in my mind that having 'IT ALL' all does not mean that I must be a slave to what society dictates 'IT ALL' to be. Unfortunately, that is what society means by 'having it all' and that is what I am arguing against.

Some individuals argue that it is possible for women to have it all but not at the same time. It is postulated that different things in a woman's life may be achieved at different times.

To me that is exactly demonstrating the point that you cannot have it all. 'Having it all' suggests having it all concurrently. If that is not possible then it means we cannot 'have it all'. Life has shown us that it is absurd to expect and impossible to have a successful family life concurrently with a successful professional life without something 'giving'.

In a successful woman's life, there are invariably significant sacrifices which means that there is something weathering in the undercurrent. That is, something somewhere is being sacrificed and if that is the case then a woman is not having it all.

This does not mean that she may not be having a reasonable, or even excellent quality of life. However, it is about acknowledging that this is at the expense of something else; it is always a balancing act. Many also argue that having it all means that a woman, can or should, like a man, be able to achieve all that she desires in society without having to make compromises that are not similarly expected of men. For example, statistics have shown that a man can expect to climb the career ladder and fulfil his career aspirations between the ages of mid 20s to late 30s without taking a career break.

In my experience, certainly in medicine, this is not necessarily the case for a woman who is expected to take a career break if she desires to have children and especially if she intends to be the primary caregiver to her children. This, on the other hand, is not automatically expected of a man.

When this is equally expected of a man or when it becomes a given that both a man and a woman in a relationship will share these responsibilities and career interruptions equally in bringing up a family, then it could be said that indeed a woman can have it all. Our reality today is not the default position I just described; hence, by virtue of biology and society's norms, there is a natural obstacle for a woman achieving success and all she desires concurrently.

Regardless of this reality, however, society puts a lot of pressure on women to demonstrate the ability to achieve all the things that men have traditionally achieved - that is, to excel in their career as well as

Chapter 15

keeping it all together at home. This includes being always immaculately groomed, manicured and well turned out as well as being amicable and well liked whilst at the same time being firm and taking the lead in the boardroom. On the other hand, no one bats an eyelid if a man is not the most approachable person and is even aggressive in the boardroom. It is deemed manly and is, in fact, what is expected.

This is a difficult dichotomy for a woman to negotiate. She is expected to be soft and likeable but not concurrently the hard-faced leader who shows few or no emotions, regardless of what she may be facing at work or quietly undergoing at home. She must always 'keep it together', otherwise she has failed. Some have contended that to state that women cannot have it all is to deny women and in particular, younger women and young girls their dreams to aspire to become whatever they desire to become.

It is felt that by saying women cannot have it all it is synonymous with saying to young girls, "Do not dare to dream, do not dare to burst through the glass ceiling. Your options are limited, and you can only achieve limited goals." Moreover, it is argued that saying a woman cannot have it all is akin to society denying her what her creator has endowed her with and made available for her.

In my opinion, this is far from being the case. Both are not mutually exclusive. As I demonstrated in my own life, I dared to dream, I dared to embrace with both arms what has been handed to me by my maker. I shot for THE moon and dare I say, landed on MY moon. However, this did come at a price and at no point was I able to say truly that I was totally fulfilled both in my professional life as well as in my personal life concurrently, especially when I decided to start a family, including starting to have children. At some point there were sacrifices made.

For example, I did not spend as much time as I would have liked with my children when they were at a younger age. As a case in point, I had three weeks off after the birth of my second child before I returned to university. This meant leaving my baby with someone for them to provide the care that I would have normally provided 24 hours, seven days a week. I was significantly blessed with someone who was a true mother figure and provided my child with untold love, comfort and care.

However, this was not ideal. Many would even frown significantly upon this. However, that was the price that I had to pay - more importantly the price that I was prepared to pay to achieve my goal of completing my degree within a specified time. Thank God my child does not appear to have suffered as a result of that decision but someone, somewhere, may argue otherwise! So, it is with a

Chapter 15

resounding 'No' that I answer my question, "Can women have it all?" It is possible to achieve your goals sequentially in seasons but never everything concurrently. During the process, something will suffer, something must give, something will be sacrificed. The important thing is for us as women to be cognisant of this and make a deliberate decision as to what it is that we wish to sacrifice at any given time and be prepared to manage or live with the consequence. In essence, we must be HONEST, FLEXIBLE, PATIENT...and, unapologetically, BE OURSELVES!

I think it is crucial that women who have achieved much, and in the eye of a younger woman looking on appear to have achieved it all, be open and honest and tell the narrative of what is really happening. Let us talk about the sacrifices that it took and the things we had to forgo.

For it is unhelpful and, I dare say, hypocritical, to give the impression that we are oh-so-successful, and we can have it all. This creates unreal expectations and potentially puts unnecessary stress on younger, unsuspecting women to achieve the impossible when all that needs to be said is that you cannot have it all. At least, not concurrently - and certainly not without some area of your life 'suffering'. That, however, in no way precludes success and a beautiful and fulfilled life.

CAN WOMEN HAVE IT ALL?

Some, e.g. Olajumoke Adenowa, an African architect and entrepreneur, argue that it should not even be a case that this question be even asked. It is argued that it is chauvinistic and framing, offensive and unfair that this question gets asked of women when it is not equally asked of men. That, therefore, negates the question. She further argues that asking such a question is like questioning God about why he gave a woman a brain and a womb.

Ola argues that a woman, like a man, is born with a purpose and it is her responsibility and right to sense that purpose and pursue it. If that takes her outside of the home, then so be it. She argues strongly that form follows function, and therefore the way you were created and came into the world follows the function that you were supposed to fulfil. So, if a woman was just supposed to have children, she would have come into this world with a womb and a partial brain to cope with childcare only, and not the dexterous brain that is capable of taking the same exams which men take at universities.

I totally agree with Ola and support the arguments that she puts forth in defence of women being treated equally to men by society. However, the fact is that this age-old question has been asked for many years and will and should continue to be asked. Like many topics surrounding women's empowerment and women's rights, this and many

Chapter 15

similar questions will continue to form the fabric of our society, being one of the key issues that needs to be constantly debated. If answering the question allows us to debate the relevant issues and allows for different perspectives and, hopefully, frankness and truth, then let us continue to ask and deconstruct this and similar questions in a quest to empower women, hold relevant authorities accountable, including governments and religious organisations, and bring about necessary changes.

Oprah Winfrey talks about living for the 'ALONG'. That message is in keeping with what we were constantly told at medical school as we yearned desperately to complete our training and become fully-fledged doctors. "Enjoy the journey," we were repeatedly told.

It is about enjoying and being the best version of yourself at any given time in your life, rather than waiting for the ultimate culmination when you 'arrive' at some imaginable pinnacle and can declare that you "have it all". In the process it is about standing for something larger than yourself and giving something back. It is about service to others rather than having it all.

We would do well to take our cue from King Solomon. He was the third King of ancient Israel and is credited as the wisest man that ever lived. Having chased all there is to find and explore in life, trying to find meaning and satisfaction in life, he repeatedly emphasized that we ought to enjoy what we are able to enjoy during life's trajectory (Ecclesiastes 2:24; 9:9-10) but he concluded ultimately, in Ecclesiastes 12:13, that human beings cannot live meaningful lives without God. King Solomon was also the great and wise promoter of seasons – Ecclesiastes 3:1-8. It is a fact that we will have seasons in our lives; it is one of life's enduring principles (Genesis 8:22). Therefore, we cannot have everything concurrently. There cannot be adequate sunshine in winter for a plant to sprout or bud. Even if we try to create the sunlight artificially, it is not the same.

Equally, summer fruits that are canned, frozen, pickled or preserved in some other way may be eaten in winter but, let us face it, they will never be the same fresh berries that we naturally pluck and enjoy directly from the trees or vines at the height of the summer months. So how are things stacking up for me?

Despite the crises that have become a natural part of the landscape of my life, I can confidently and categorically state that I have achieved success and will continue to do so throughout the rest of my life! In some ways it is quite exciting to anticipate the unravelling of the various areas of my life.

Chapter 15

For example, I am eager to see my children's success, and to realise the outcome of the investments that I continue to make in myself, including looking after my physical health and wellbeing as well as into my spiritual, social and academic development. I am also keen to realise the fruits of my investments into my treasured relationships and friendships.

I have learnt to manage crises successfully but could do with a reprieve at this point. Will I be granted one? For now, I am embracing ALL that I have been BLESSED with! However, I also know that it will be well, regardless of whatever else pops us because I am made to last!

CAN WOMEN HAVE IT ALL?

"Can Women Have it all? No. We are always striving! It is impossible to maintain a perpetual state of equilibrium ... on this earth. However, this in no way prevents a woman from attaining her highest potential and enjoying an excellent life which is happy, even joyful - and totally fulfilling."

"Have you enjoyed this book?

I hope you have, but even if not, perhaps it has challenged your thinking; your perspective or your attitude.

Maybe you've even been inspired.

Why not leave a review on the platform where you purchased the book?

Let's keep the conversation going.

I would be MOST GRATEFUL. xx"

Printed in Great Britain
by Amazon

21257303R00149